# The Art of the Russian MATRYOSHKA

# The Art of the Russian MATRYOSHKA

Rett Ertl and Rick Hibberd

Vernissage

Vernissage Press, LLC, Boulder, Colorado

*Published by
Vernissage Press, LLC
2200 Central Avenue
Boulder, Colorado 80301
(888) 849-8697 • info@vernissagepress.com
www.vernissagepress.com*

*Designed by Rick Hibberd
Edited by Gail Buyske and Jody Berman
Photography by Rick Hibberd, Yakov Chitov, Denis Tolstoy*

*ISBN 0-9725027-1-8*

*Library of Congress Control Number 2002094629*

*Printed and bound in Hong Kong
by Dai Nippon Printing Company,(Hong Kong) Ltd.
10 9 8 7 6 5 4 3 2 1*

*Plate: 003
Factory: Sergievskaya Igrushka, Sergiev Posad
This design is a copy of the first Russian-made matryoshka, created in 1899. As on the original doll, the features are outlined by wood burning.*

*Frontispiece, Plate: 001
City: Raduzhnoye
Finished dolls join works in progress on
Natasha Pugaeva's work table.*

*Title page, Plate: 002
Factory: Semyonovskaya Rospis, Semyonov
Size: 18-piece, 12 inches tall*

This book is dedicated to the Russian artists,
craftspeople, and entrepreneurs who keep
the matryoshka doll alive today.

And to Tania and Galina
who showed us the wonders of Russia

# Contents

# Acknowledgements

Plate: 004 (opposite)
*City: Raduzhnoye*
*A box in a studio containing work in progress makes a richly colored still life.*

I WAS ENCOURAGED to write this book by my friend Rick Hibberd, a designer who lived in Moscow with his wife, Gail Buyske, from 1998 to 2001. Rick suggested the project to me because of my involvement in Russian crafts. He also brought the vision and the know-how to the project that turned the idea into a reality.

Gail also participated actively in this project. Besides continually offering moral support, she contributed extensive and invaluable editorial work, especially in the final stages of production.

*The Art of the Russian Matryoshka* might never have been written without frequent comments from my friends at The Three Lynx Toy Store in Castle Rock, Colorado. The store owner, Vicki Miller, has one of the the best matryoshka collections in the United States. She frequently urged me to write this book. Her employee Bev Larsen, who has one of the best collections of Turnip matryoshki, just assumed that I would do so.

In writing Chapter 1 on the history of matryoshka production, I consulted the books listed in the Bibliography, but also commissioned papers from three Russian authorities. Some historical perspective was provided by Aleksandr Bianki, who is one of Russia's leading experts on Russian wooden toys; several of the specific facts came from Aleksandr Grekov, the director of the Artistic-Pedagogical Museum of Toys of the Russian Academy of Education; and most of the history, especially of Sergiev Posad, was provided by Svetlana Gorozhanina, the director of the Museum of Russian Applied Folk Art of the Eighteenth through the Twentieth Centuries of the Trinity-Sergiev Monastery. I had the pleasure of spending time with Aleksandr Bianki and Svetlana Gorozhanina. I am not only grateful for their contributions to this book, but thoroughly enjoyed my visits with them.

Thanks are also due to editor Jody Berman, who patiently monitored and corrected my writing and to John Hausman of TolsToys, whose attention to business gave me the time for it all.

*Plate: 005*
*Factory: Sergievskaya Igrushka, Sergiev Posad*
*Traditional Sergiev Posad dolls line the shelves,ready to be sold.*

# AUTHOR'S NOTE

THE WORD *MATRYOSHKA* is related to the Russian word *mat'*, meaning "mother." The symbolism is obvious, as each doll has one daughter inside, and then another. However, *matryoshka* is not a form of the word *mat'*. Such a related word, *matushka* (literally, "little mother") does exist, but it generally refers to the wife of a Russian Orthodox priest. "Matryoshka" is actually the diminutive form of the name "Matryona," a relatively common name in rural Russia in the nineteenth century.

Искусство Русской
МАТРЁШКИ

*Plate: 006*
*In Russian, the title of the book does not have the article* The, *nor the preposition* of.
*I've included a setting of the title here, just for flavor.*

In Russian, the word *matryoshka* stands on its own, so the addition of the word *doll* is an English explanatory term. Because Russian uses the Cyrillic alphabet, many words can be spelled several different ways in English. *Matryoshka* is one such word. The Russian letter that is pronounced "yo" is written with an "e" with an umlaut (ë). The most common spelling of *matryoshka* (other than the one we are using) is *matreshka*, but it is also often written *matrioshka*.

No matter how you spell the word, it is hard to say. The "yo" sound following an "r" is one of the most difficult to pronounce. Usually Americans pronounce the word "mah-TROOSH-kah," and I tell non-Russian speakers to use that pronunciation. It is incorrect, however, to call them babushka dolls or matushka dolls or nanochka dolls. A *babushka* (grandmother), as we shall see, is a particular type of matryoshka doll.

There are several English terms for these dolls as well. Most commonly, they are called nesting dolls, but many people call them stacking dolls or even pull-em-apart dolls. Throughout the book, I use the following terms interchangeably: matryoshka, matryoshka doll, and nesting doll. The Russian plural of matryoshka is matryoshki, and I use that term rather than the Anglicized "matryoshkas."

When I began this book, I thought of matryoshki as representing motherhood and fertility, not just because of the symbolism of a woman bearing children, but also because of the Russian wooden eggs to which they are related. Furthermore, both motherhood and fertility are closely tied in Russian culture to the concept of Russia itself. I have completed the book by concluding that matryoshki embody many themes: they themselves are symbols within symbols.

*Plate: 007*
*City: Kirov*
*To get to the Art Alliance factory in Kirov, head south out of town, then turn right just after the bus stop with a matryoshka painted on it.*

# Preface

I FIRST TRAVELED TO THE SOVIET UNION in 1971 after graduating from college. I was fascinated by the four-inch, 9-piece doll that I saw in a *Beriozka* store, one of a state-run chain of shops that only accepted foreign currency. I bought it and there it all began. At that time, matryoshka dolls were quite uniform. Almost all of them had five or six pieces and were five or six inches tall. The colors were generally similar among dolls and the forms were relatively consistent. But each variation in color and form represented a region. A few cities had factories that produced matryoshki and dolls could be distinguished by the factory that produced them. Some of the factories that operated in the 1970s and 1980s are still operating, and most are described in this book. Several factories have since closed.

Since that first trip in 1971, I have visited the Soviet Union and later Russia over forty times. After the fall of the Soviet Union in 1991, the variety of nesting dolls exploded. The first matryoshka that departed strikingly from the old tradition was the "Gorby" doll, depicting General Secretary Mikhail Gorbachev and several of his predecessors. Artists have since become increasingly creative and now nesting dolls come in a diverse array of sizes, shapes, and designs.

*Plate: 008*
*Title: Gorby Doll*
*Size: 5-piece, 8 inches tall*
*Collection: Rett and Tania Ertl*
*The author's first acquisition after the fall of the Soviet Union, this doll features a knot in the wood in the place of the birthmark on Mikhail Gorbachev's head.*

Years later, I started a company called TolsToys and began to import gift items from Russia. At first I focused on wooden toys, especially the chicks that peck as they are rotated on a paddle-type board. But when I put nesting dolls next to the toys so that people would know the toys were Russian, people insisted on buying the nesting dolls.

After the first few trips to Russia, I saw a matryoshka factory in operation. Shortly thereafter, I started to work with Denis Tolstoy, a grandson of one of the Soviet Union's best known writers, Alexei Tolstoy (a distant relative of Leo Tolstoy). Denis has been with me ever since as our representative in Russia. By 1998, he was able to buy a car. His Opel has become a valuable asset for our business (and for this book).

There are several books on nesting dolls, and they are listed in the bibliography along with a brief description. The ones that were published in Russia are short, inexpensively printed, and translated from Russian by Russians. I decided to write *The Art of the Russian Matryoshka* to present nesting dolls from an western perspective and in native English. There is one American book about nesting dolls, *A Collector's Guide to Nesting Dolls* by Michele Lyons Lefkovitz. It is a good book for collectors of Soviet-era matryoshki, but it is out of print and its photographs are almost all black and white.

As an importer, wholesaler, and retailer of matryoshka dolls, I have been impressed by the desire of many collectors for more information—how the dolls are made, who makes them, and so on. My two main goals in writing the book were to explain how nesting dolls are made and to provide the best possible photographs of matryoshka dolls. *The Art of the Russian Matryoshka* is an attempt to bring nesting dolls alive.

For those who are fascinated by these dolls, this book is intended to be a guide, following the dolls' journey from linden log to the outside world.

Rett Ertl

# 1

# A History

## From Japanese Doll to Symbol of Russia

# A History
## From Japanese Doll to Symbol of Russia

Matryoshka dolls are a relatively new phenomenon in the context of Russian history. Russian matryoshki first appeared in 1899 in the city of Sergiev Posad, about 50 kilometers north of Moscow. The generally accepted story is that a nesting doll was brought to Russia from Japan by a Russian traveller, probably a merchant. The first Russian matryoshki were made during this same period, but it is not known whether this was a coincidence or the result of the Japanese influence. In any case, matryoshki were introduced into a fertile artistic soil and a long tradition of woodworking. Once the seeds were planted, village artists quickly nurtured matryoshki into becoming the symbol of Russia that they are today.

For centuries, the Sergiev Posad region has been known for its folk art. To this day, neighboring villages such as Abramtsevo, Khotkovo, and Bogorodskoye enjoy a similar reputation. Legend has it that the first Sergiev Posad toy was made in the thirteenth century by St. Sergius of Radonezh, for whom the city was named, and who founded the most important landmark in Sergiev Posad, the Trinity-Sergiev Monastery. Whether or not that legend is true, the early Sergiev Posad toys were typically carved renditions of animals or people, often brightly painted. Records show that the tsar's children received toys from Sergiev Posad as early as 1628. Visitors to the monastery bought toys for their children, much as visitors to museums today buy gifts in museum gift shops.

*Plate: 009 (chapter title)*
*City: Sergiev Posad*
*Visitors to the Trinity-Sergiev Monastery bought toys to take home as early as the 17th century. This picture from the 1920s shows an active market.*

*Plate: 010 (opposite, above)*
*A street in Sergiev Posad, c. 1910.*

### Russia's Toy Center

By 1880, there were 322 toy workshops in Sergiev Posad, of which 156 worked with papier-mâché or mastic; 43 made carved wooden toys; 28 turned toys on a lathe; and 95 worked with a variety of materials. There were fourteen toy stores in the city and two wholesale warehouses. To assist the craftsmen of Sergiev Posad, in 1885

*Plate: 011 (opposite, below)*
*Title: The First Matryoshka*
*Collection: Artistic-Pedagogical Museum of Toys, Sergiev Posad*
*The first matryoshka, painted by Sergei Malyutin in 1899. The smallest doll is an infant, thus accentuating the fertility theme.*

*Plate: 012 (above)*
*City: Sergiev Posad*
*In this undated photo from early in the 1900s, workers paint carved animals, and wooden heads that were affixed to cloth dolls.*

*Plate: 013 (above)*
*City: Sergiev Posad*
*Artists and teachers from the Zemstvo Toy and Art Workshop in Sergiev Posad, 1912. In the first row, left to right: Shukaev, N. P. Komarov, V. I. Ryzhkov, M. I. Zimin, M. A. Chvatov, V. D. Pichugin, M. E. Korotkov; Standing, left to right: I. A. Tolstukhin, V. A. Aleksandrov, K. A. Ryzhkov, V. I. Borutskii, S. I. Tokarev, E. I. Shumikhin.*

*Plate 014 (left)*
*Title: Portrait of Savva Mamontov, 1887*
*Artist: Valentin Serov*
*Collection: The Picture Gallery, Odessa, Ukraine*

the Moscow District Council opened the Trade and Industry Museum of Handcrafted Items, also known as the Folk Art Museum. This museum, located in Moscow, was to be a coordinating organization for the craftsmen of the Moscow *guberniya* (the equivalent of an American state), modeled after similar organizations in western Europe. As one of the centers of handcrafted art, Sergiev Posad would be the beneficiary of several of the museum's decisions to support the development of regional crafts.

The district council opened an educational toy workshop in 1891. Five years later, Sergei

Morozov, a major donor to the Folk Art Museum, constructed a building to house this workshop. Morozov was a wealthy merchant whose cousin Ivan was known for bringing the works of the western European impressionists to Russia. (The Morozov mansion in Moscow, located near the Kremlin, now houses the Pushkin Museum.)

In 1896, the workshop had fifteen masters and ten students. After their education, the students would return home to practice their craft.

## Nineteenth Century Russia

To understand the origin of the matryoshka, it helps to understand what was occurring in nineteenth-century Russia. There was an intellectual undercurrent that generally opposed the harshness of tsarist rule. This undercurrent manifested itself in the extreme with the assassination of Tsar Alexander II in 1881 in St. Petersburg. On an intellectual level, this dissatisfaction can be seen in the novels of Ivan Turgenev and Leo Tolstoy. Turgenev's *Fathers and Sons* shows the struggle between a father who represents the old world, in which servants are treated as inferiors, and a son who represents the new world, in which the servants are treated as human beings. Often, liberals in nineteenth-century Russia looked upon peasants as people who were not only equal but even superior to the nobleman. The character Platon Karataev in Tolstoy's *War and Peace* is perhaps the best known example of the nobility's tendency to endow an ignorant peasant with an innate wisdom.

Parallel with the nobility's increased interest in the peasantry, however, traditional folk art was suffering from increasing industrialization. The work of master craftsmen was being replaced by industrial production and, in some cases, by inexpensive imitations. Not only were the villages losing their cultural heritage, but the craftsmen were being put out of work. It was at this time that people started to perceive objects of traditional peasant culture as works of art. Prior to that, peasants had painted utilitarian objects such as spoons, bowls, or trays as a hobby, and city people did not especially value their work.

It is against this background that the Russian nobility of the late nineteenth century supported art in general and the art of the village in particular.

## Art and Technology

As Russia became more industrialized, the nobility looked for ways to combine traditional art with new technology. They wanted to support the work of the villages, where the master craftsmen lived. As one example, new sewing machine technology, which had been developed in the cities, was transferred to the villages so that embroidery could be done there.

The development of the matryoshka is arguably the most successful of these efforts to combine technology with folk culture. As noted earlier, it is generally believed that the first matryoshka was brought to Russia from Japan by a traveller or merchant. One could say, therefore,

*Plate: 015 (above, top)*
*City: Sergiev Posad*
*The painting room of the RKKA artel, which later became Factory No. 1. The workshop director Mr. Uvarov is on the left. From the archives of the Artistic-Pedagogical Museum of Toys.*

*Plate: 016 (above, bottom)*
*City: Sergiev Posad*
*The warehouse of a company called* Koverkustexport *in Sergiev Posad, 1920s. Judging from its name, this company was an exporter of rugs and craft items.*

that production of matryoshki in Russia was imposed on the "people" by aristocrats. But, had it not been for a long tradition of woodworking in the Russian villages, it is unlikely that matryoshki would have found such enthusiastic acceptance and development. In fact, Russian lathe operators had been making nesting Easter eggs for years. They had also been producing a game called *biryulki*, which is a cross between tiddlywinks and pick-up sticks that is played with a variety of small wooden objects that are generally round and turned on a lathe. These game pieces had been produced in Russia since at least the early nineteenth century. So the production of matryoshki was a natural progression for Russian lathe operators.

Among the sponsors of local artists were Savva and Elizaveta Mamontov. Their families owned railroads and textile factories and an estate called Abramtsevo, not far from Sergiev Posad, where they supported the work of fine artists. These included many of the "Itinerant" school of painters that has come to be considered the renaissance of Russian art. Among the artists who came to Abramtsevo were Viktor Vasnetsov, Ilya Repin, Valentin Serov, and Mikhail Vrubel. The art school at Abramtsevo is still producing well trained artists, some of whom are using their talents to create matryoshki. Savva Mamontov's brother, Anatoly, also wished to support the peasantry; he did so by founding a Moscow toy workshop,

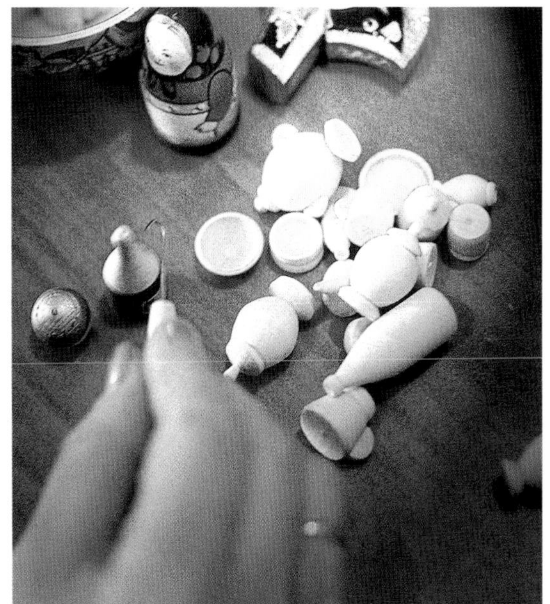

*Plate: 017 (above)*
*City: Sergiev Posad*
*The catalog/price list of the Zemstvo Toy and Art Workshop in Sergiev Posad. It appears that the numbers above the matryoshki are item numbers; the numbers on the shelves are presumably the prices.*

*Plate: 018 (left)*
*Factory: Sergievskaya Igrushka, Sergiev Posad*
*Popular throughout the 19th century, the game of* biryulki *indicates that the art of turning was highly developed well before the first matryoshka was turned in 1899. The game involves players picking up these pieces with a hooked instrument and dropping them into a cup.*

Children's Education (*Detskoye Vospitanie*).

In the late 1890s, a nesting doll from Japan appeared at the Children's Education workshop. This doll consisted of five nested pieces and was shaped like a cylinder, rounded off on the top. It pictured a monk named Fukuruma, who had gone to the forest to meditate and sat so long that he reputedly lost the use of his arms and legs. This doll is still on display at the Sergiev Posad Museum of Toys.

It is generally accepted, although not documented, that the first Russian-made matryoshka doll was painted by Sergei Malyutin, a peasant who had risen to become the head of the Abramtsevo workshop. The lathe work was done by Vasilii Zvyozdochkin, an employee of the Children's Education workshop, who came from a long line of lathe operators from Podolsk, an area south of Moscow which was well known for its nesting Easter eggs. Zvyozdochkin became known as the best lathe operator in Sergiev Posad.

*Plate: 019*
*Title: Fukuruma (c.1898)*
*City: Sergiev Posad*
*Artist: Unknown*
*Size: 7-piece, 6.8 inches tall*
*Collection: Artistic-Pedagogical Museum of Toys*
*This Japanese nested doll may have been the inspiration for the first matryoshka.*

Zvyozdochkin's memoirs do not mention the Japanese doll; he describes how, in 1899, he and two other lathe operators came up with the idea of a lathe-turned wooden doll depicting a person because Anatoly Mamontov was constantly asking for new toys. The first doll that was made by Zvyozdochkin did not open. Zvyozdochkin's colleagues suggested that he hollow it out and put more dolls inside. This he did, and the first matryoshka appeared – an 8-piece doll.

Zvyozdochkin writes that his doll was taken to be painted in Arbat, a center of artistry in central Moscow. Perhaps Malyutin, who was also actively engaged in stage design, was in Moscow at the time. The design features a girl in a national costume, holding various small objects in her hands—a chicken, a basket, a bundle, a scarf. The original doll was matte with wood burned outlines and the colors were somewhat dark, especially compared to the many bright matryoshki seen today.

*Plate: 020*
*City: Sergiev Posad*
*Men and boys alike painted matryoshki in the 1920s.*
*At that time it was primarily a male endeavor.*

Zvyozdochkin was to spend the rest of his life teaching craftsmen to make matryoshki; he was an instructor at the Professional Technical School in Sergiev Posad from 1913 to 1941.

Were Sergei Malyutin and Vasilii Zvyodochkin inspired by a Japanese doll brought to Russia by a traveler, or was it just a coincidence that the Japanese doll dates to the same era? This may never be conclusively determined. In either case, the matryoshka was a logical step in the progression of the Russian woodworking tradition, and has gone on to create a proud tradition of its own.

## Beginnings of an Art Form

The first matryoshki consisted of three, six, and eight pieces. For some reason, the early dolls depicted what appears to be a family without a father. They include males, but those males are clearly children. After Zvyozdochkin and Malyutin produced the first matryoshka doll, the Children's

*Plate: 021 (below, top)*
*City: Sergiev Posad*
*Artist: I. G. Prokhorov*
*Collection: Artistic-Pedagogical Museum of Toys*
Bogatyrs, *Russian knights-errant.*

*Plate: 022 (below, bottom)*
*City: Sergiev Posad*
*Artist: V. I. Sokolov*
*Collection: Museum of Applied Folk Art*
*Bottle-shaped doll, early 1900s.*

Education workshop produced matryoshki in Moscow until 1904. That year, all of the assets of Children's Education were transferred to a workshop in Sergiev Posad. Thus Sergiev Posad became, and still is, the center of matryoshka production in Russia.

In 1900, one of the first dolls was taken to Paris for an exhibition. It was received enthusiastically and even received an award. Then in 1904, the workshops received a large matryoshka order from Paris, providing the stimulus for many of Sergiev Posad's artists and lathe operators to turn their attention to the making of matryoshka dolls. The matryoshki thus became simpler, more folk-oriented, and less expensive; the price fell by as much as twenty times. At the same time, the main theme became the female figure, and especially the peasant figure in peasant costume.

Among the masters of Sergiev Posad was N. D. Bartram, who was a well-known artist before he turned to matryoshki. His works often depicted heroes from fairy tales, Russians in their regional costume, and literary characters. In 1909, Bartram created a series of matryoshki based on the works of the Russian author Nikolai Gogol, to commemorate the centenary of the author's birth. In 1910, Bartram brought together eleven experienced artists in an *artel,* a combination cooperative and workshop; some of the work is done at home, some at the *artel.* It was called Handcraft Artist (in Russian, *Kustar Khudozhnik*). Another *artel,* the Partnership of Kaplen's Descendants, which had been in existence since the late nineteenth century, employed thirty-two masters and ten apprentices. Many of the artists were from families of icon painters from the Trinity-Sergiev Monastery. One of the more well known was the Pichugin family.

Matryoshka dolls began to be made in a variety of shapes and with a variety of themes. There were cone-shaped dolls, bottle-shaped dolls, and dolls with pointed heads. Some dolls took on the shape of the subjects they depicted. The Russian *bogatyrs,* knights-errant whose exploits were described in Russian legends known as *byliny,* wore their traditional pointed hats. Matryoshka themes ranged from characters in famous novels to more common fairy tale scenes. Interestingly, many of the themes that are popular on modern matryoshki—political figures, fairy tales, and peasant families—which are considered new, were in fact subjects of some of the earliest matryoshki.

## Revolution

As the revolution approached in Russia, there were hundreds of artists making nesting dolls in Sergiev Posad. By 1911, the city had 41 matryoshka workshops. Most, but not all, had lathe operators who turned blanks for matryoshki. All had artists who painted the dolls.

Like much artistic activity, matryoshka making continued strong for several years after the revolution of 1917. Toys were no longer imported, so domestic toys became more widespread and master craftsmen continued with their work. In 1918, a toy museum opened in Sergiev Posad. In 1922, a Regional Handcrafters' Union was created. The union's Russian name is *Raikustpromsoyuz,* an early example of a tongue-twisting Soviet acronym. This union coordinated the *artels* of the city. In 1926, the union worked with six *artels,* combining the talents of 260 craftsmen.

During this period, matryoshka painting in Sergiev Posad became more uniform. What we now call the traditional Sergiev Posad matryoshka came into existence in the mid-1920s. It was roughly based on the first matryoshka painted by Sergei Malyutin, featuring a girl in a national costume, sometimes holding a small object in her hands—a chicken, a basket, a bundle, a scarf. The matte, dark feeling of the original was brightened up, and the wood burned outlines were replaced with painted contours.

One of the artists who played a major role in the establishment of this particular matryoshka design was V. I. Sokolov. His matryoshki of the early 1920s depicted anti-clerical and anti-imperialistic themes (for example, "Satire on a Priest" and "God Is Capital"), which, presumably, set him in good stead with the Bolshevik authorities. He participated in exhibits organized by the Sergiev Posad branch of the Association of Artists of Revolutionary Russia, which was formed in 1925, and was for a time chairman of that organization.

*Plate: 023 (below)*
*City: Sergiev Posad*
*A member of one of the best known families of matryoshka artists, V. D. Pichugin.*

## The Soviet Period

When Josef Stalin consolidated his hold on the government in the late 1920s, the matryoshka doll, like other forms of art, became the victim of political heavy-handedness. The many *artels* and workshops that had formed in the years since 1900 were combined into one: the Sergiev Posad Handcraft-Industrial Artel. Artists no longer had the freedom to paint any nesting doll they wanted. On the contrary, they were told what they could produce and were soon limited to painting the traditional peasant girls.

In 1930, the city of Sergiev Posad was renamed Zagorsk to rid the name of its religious reference, and the name of the *artel* was lengthened; it became the Workers' and Peasants' Red Army Zagorsk Handcraft-Industrial Artel, or, using its

*Plate: 024 (below)*
*City: Sergiev Posad*
*V. I. Sokolov, one of the most influential matryoshka painters of the 1920s.*

Russian initials, the RKKA Artel. The *artel* exported 15 to 20 percent of its production. Even in the 1930s, after years of local production, the *artel* bought many of its blanks for export-quality matryoshki from the Podolsk area, south of Moscow, from which lathe operator Zvyozdochkin had hailed. Eventually, several of the lathe operators from Babenki, near Podolsk, were invited to live and work in Zagorsk. In 1960, the RKKA became state property and was renamed Factory No. 1.

In 1944, even as World War II was raging, a second workshop was opened. It was called the Zagorsk Artistic-Production Workshop and has since become the factory called Souvenir. World War II is still known in Russia as the Great Patriotic War, and apparently authorities thought there should be another producer of what had already become a symbol of Russian culture. Soldiers were even called back from the war to make matryoshki and other Russian handcrafts.

Shortly after the war, in 1947, a third workshop was opened, this one called the Factory of Toys and Cultural Items. That factory is now AOFIS, the Joint Stock Factory of Toys and Souvenirs. All of the Sergiev Posad factories continue to exist today and are described in Chapter 5.

*Plate: 025*
*City: Sergiev Posad*
*A couple painting matryoshki in their apartment, dated in the 1930s. This photo is interesting from two standpoints: no private enterprise was allowed during the Soviet period, so there should not have been any home painters in the 1930s; and the presence of the large icon in the corner in Stalin's Russia is unusual.*

The activities at Sergiev Posad spawned other matryoshka-producing centers. Historically, much of Russia's commercial activity has occurred along the Volga River. The main stimulus for the expansion of matryoshka production to other cities and villages seems to have been the centuries-old market in the city of Nizhny Novgorod, the major city on the Volga, about 300 miles east of Moscow. (Like Sergiev Posad, Nizhny Novgorod was renamed for much of the Soviet period. It was called Gorky from 1932 until the early 1990s.) Craftsmen from Merinovo, near Semyonov, about 50 miles north of Nizhny Novgorod and from Maidan, about 100 miles south of Nizhny Novgorod, may have brought examples of nesting dolls from the market to their villages. These villages then began to produce matryoshki with their own distinctive features.

Finally, matryoshki appeared in Vyatka (now Kirov), which today is the farthest north and east of any of the major nesting doll production centers. As in Sergiev Posad, artists and craftsmen in Semyonov, Maidan, and Vyatka were gathered into local factories in about 1930. Each of these centers developed its own style, with some of the dolls produced in eastern cities looking distinctly Asian. The city of Semyonov, which combined the talents of many artists from several villages in the late 1920s, is now the largest producer of nesting dolls in Russia, with two factories producing thousands of matryoshki every month.

Even when there was not much room for creativity, each doll was handmade, and therefore no two were identical. Only a small percentage of the matryoshki made in the Soviet period varied from the norm. Michele Lyons Lefkovitz's book, *A Collector's Guide to Nesting Dolls,* shows warriors and gnomes, illustrating some unusual themes and shapes. Yet in the sixty years from 1930 to 1990, the vast majority of dolls from each of the matryoshka-producing cities was very similar in shape and color. For example, a large percentage of the Semyonov dolls was painted on a yellow background. They all depicted a peasant woman in a scarf and all of the dolls inside were in the same style and with the same subject as the outside doll.

In Kirov in the 1960s, artists began to glue small pieces of rye straw onto their matryoshki in geometrical or flower shapes. Kirov is a center of wooden box production, another traditional art form, and some of those boxes are decorated with rye straw. Kirov's matryoshka artists rightly decided that this straw could add to the appeal of their dolls. This tradition continues in the Kirov and Nolinsk factories.

*Plate: 026*
*City: Sergiev Posad*
*Collection: Artistic-Pedagogical Museum of Toys*
*An unidentified artist at The Workers' and Peasants' Red Army Artel (RKKA) paints a matryoshka, 1930s.*

## An Explosion of Styles and Themes

Two unsanctioned art sales areas appeared in parks on the outskirts of Moscow in the late 1980s—Bitsevsky Park and Izmailovsky Park. One of the slogans of the perestroika period was *glasnost*—openness—and these beginning markets were allowed to continue to operate.

An even more surprising sign of the times was the imaginative and sometimes politically relevant—and irreverent—work that was allowed to be sold in the parks. The appearance of the "Gorby" doll, depicting Gorbachev on the outside and his predecessors on the inside, not only marked a break with officially controlled matryoshka production; it also indicated that political satire was back in the public domain.

The market that started near Izmailovsky Park has evolved to become Russia's primary sales center for matryoshka dolls, both at its wholesale market on Wednesdays and its retail market on the weekends. The market began with a few artists showing their paintings outside the wall of the Izmailovsky Monastery. It was known as the *vernissage*, a word denoting the opening of an art show. As the market grew, it moved across the street into Izmailovsky Park and then, in 1990, into its present location outside the Izmailovo Stadium. In the early days the market witnessed frequent turf battles as the sellers, who were often the artists themselves, were punished for not paying their dues or for occupying the wrong spaces. Today the Izmailovo market is a well regulated business with hundreds of booths selling everything from matryoshka dolls to icons to World War II gear to Christmas tree ornaments. The market continues to grow larger and evolve.

Perhaps because of the system in which they grew up, Russian artists were not particularly creative at first, and the Gorby doll was widely copied. Soon Boris Yeltsin replaced Gorbachev on the outside doll, and now Vladimir Putin has taken Yeltsin's place. But, as Soviet history recedes, artists have discovered that they are limited only by their imagination. Some of the most impressive dolls are being made by artists from the Vasnetsov School of Art in Abramtsevo, where the matryoshka had some of its earliest roots. Some feature whimsical illustrations, evoking early twentieth-century Russian artists such as Marc Chagall and Kasimir Malevich. Many of the Abramtsevo matryoshki have religious themes. Most of the matryoshki featured in Elena Filippova's *Russian Matrjoshka*, and many featured in this book, were done by artists from the Abramtsevo school.

Other artists are creating dolls that illustrate Russian fairy tales, while others copy the art of lacquer boxes onto the medallions of elaborate matryoshki, usually 7- or 10-piece, but sometimes as many as 30 pieces. A new Sergiev Posad factory, Sergievskaya Igrushka (Sergiev Toy), is reproducing the first matryoshka created by Malyutin and Zvyozdochkin. And, at the other extreme, matryoshki also depict such subjects as Marilyn Monroe, Elvis Presley, Bill Clinton and his alleged girlfriends, not to mention rock groups, opera singers and Russian tsars.

It is unlikely that Vasilii Zvyozdochkin and Sergei Malyutin had any idea that their little doll would be the first of millions of matryoshki, the most popular gift purchased in Russia by visitors from around the world. Whether it be the modest 6-piece Semyonov doll or an elaborate work of art from Abramtsevo, and regardless of whether it originated in Russia or was inspired by a Japanese toy, the matryoshka has truly become a symbol of Russia at home and to the world.

## How Matryoshki are Made

# First You Take a Linden Tree

*Plate: 027 (chapter title, overleaf)*
*Title: Stacked logs*
*City: Maidan*

*Plate: 028 (above)*
*Title: Logs drying*
*City: Maidan*
*Logs can be dried horizontally, but more commonly the logs are kept vertical. The logs in the foreground are ready to be turned; the ones in the back were cut recently, and will not be ready until the following year.*

## How Matryoshki are Made

# First You Take a Linden Tree

ALTHOUGH RUSSIA has undergone two major social and economic upheavals over the past century, the technique of making matryoshki has barely changed at all. Lathe specialist Zvyozdochkin would be able to walk into any matryoshka work shop and pick up where he left off. Certainly one of the charms–and marvels–of matryoshki is how little their production has changed over the years.

A common misconception is that a nested doll is made from a single piece of wood. It is not. Each top piece and each bottom piece is cut from a separate section of the wood log. Making a matryoshka doll involves removing most of the wood from inside each doll. One cannot imagine the tool that would allow a woodworker to hollow out a piece of wood as easily as scooping out a whole egg from within its shell.

Russian nesting dolls are made of linden or birch, with the finer, hand-turned dolls being made of linden. Linden (genus *Tilia*) is a fine-grained, soft, deciduous tree. The softness makes it easy to work, and the fine grain allows it to keep its shape. Even when the dolls are imported to a dry climate, the dolls rarely crack—and only when subjected to some outside pressure. Dolls brought to the United States 30 years ago may have faded, but the wood has not cracked.

Linden is relatively common throughout the Northern Hemisphere. One of the main streets in Berlin, Unter den Linden, is named for these trees. In the western United States, where the climate is completely different from that of western Europe, the fragrant, pear-shaped linden, with its bright yellow flowers, is often the tree of choice for parkways and parking lots. There are several species of linden in the United States and Europe. In the eastern United States, some lindens are called basswood (*Tilia americana*). In England, linden trees are called limes.

Lindens are easy to identify, as there are two different leaf types on each tree. One leaf looks somewhat like a common aspen leaf, with serrated edges. The second type (called a bract) is long and thin, with a seedpod growing out of the middle of it.

Birch trees, however, are much more commonly associated with Russia and indeed are much more plentiful and less expensive than linden. Why, then, aren't most matryoshki made of birch?

*Plate: 029*
*The two types of leaves on the linden tree.*

*Plate: 030*
*Factory: Art Alliance, Kirov*
*The factory in Kirov has the most impressive log-handling operation. A crane transfers rough logs from trucks to a conveyor system, which delivers them to a multi-staged sawmill inside the factory.*

*Plate: 031*
*Factory: Art Alliance, Kirov*
*The logs come into the building, where they are stripped of their bark and sawn to the required length for splitting.*

Because birch is too hard and brittle. If a mistake is made in turning birch, the piece may break and it must be made anew. The larger dolls have proportionally thinner walls than the smaller ones, making it even more likely that birch would crack if used for such dolls. So, only small, inexpensive nesting dolls are made from birch, typically turned on automatic lathes.

## Preparing the Wood

Blank matryoshka dolls (*zagatovki* in Russian) are produced either in a factory or in a shed in someone's backyard. The larger factories are located in the cities featured in Chapter 5—Semyonov, Kirov, and Nolinsk. Some of the factories of Sergiev Posad still make blanks, but only a small number compared to the other three cities. The majority of blanks made in a backyard come from a little town, Polkhovsky Maidan, hours from the nearest city. (Pronounced my-DON, Maidan means "center" in Tartar; there are many towns in central Russia with this name. However, because only Polkhovsky Maidan is home to matryoshki, the village is referred to in this book simply as Maidan.)

There is a peculiarly Russian advantage to living near the forests, such as those near Maidan. While a person from Sergiev Posad would have to pay full price for the Maidan logs (and probably a bribe, too), a resident who lives near the forests can get them for much less than the official price.

*Plate: 032 (above)*
*Factory: Art Alliance, Kirov*
*Larger logs must be split before they can be taken to the lathe.*

*Plate: 033 (left)*
*Factory: Art Alliance, Kirov*
*The logs are rounded off on a rough lathe before they go to a finishing lathe to be turned into blanks.*

For instance, the forester may sell logs to a resident for a few bottles of vodka.

No matter where the blanks are made, the process starts in the forest. After trees are felled, their branches are removed. Then the logs must be cured, so that the nesting dolls made from them do not crack or warp. The ideal curing period is three years, but many Russian producers are using linden that has been cured for less than a year. Lathe operators in Maidan strip the bark before the drying process, and they usually dry the logs vertically, although horizontal stacks work as well if they are kept covered and have plenty of air circulation. According to the woodworkers of Maidan, if the logs are piled correctly and if the weather is warm and dry, the logs can cure in one good summer. The Maidan operators have also developed the technique of keeping the leaves on the end of the log after the bark has been removed. They say that the leaves essentially suck the moisture out of the log, thus hastening the drying process.

If the logs are cured improperly, then cracks appear, sometimes making the logs unusable. If the logs are not cured long enough and are made into dolls, the dolls will not retain their shape and may crack. Finally, if the logs are cured too long, the wood may turn brown, shrivel, and crack. One of the secrets of good blank making is to use a slightly more moist log for the top of the doll, so that when the doll is put together, the top piece shrinks to fit the bottom. If the bottom piece is moister than the top, it will later shrink and cause the top piece to be too loose. This is one of the worst defects that a matryoshka doll can have, and there is no way to correct the problem.

Once a log is properly cured, it is ready for the next step. In small Sergiev Posad factories, one or two men pull the log off the pile, carry it onto a saw, and cut it into pieces about two feet long. The worker then puts the log into a large hydraulic splitter and, depending on the diameter of the log and the size of the blank being produced, the log is split into about six pieces. The worker then places the split log onto a lathe, where he turns the rough log into a smooth round piece of wood, perhaps four inches in diameter and twenty-four inches long.

*Plate: 034*
*City: Maidan*
*Several different gouges are used in the various operations, including hollowing out the cavity, forming curves on the outside of the doll, cutting the notch where the top and bottom fit together, creating a flat base on the bottom piece, and trimming the blank from the log. As with lathe operators anywhere, the care and sharpening of the gouges is important to the craft.*

In the larger factories, this process is more automated. In Kirov, there is a complete sawmill. The logs are brought to a dock on a crane and then rolled onto a conveyor belt, which pulls the

logs into position to be cut. Rather than splitting the logs and then turning them into round logs, the workers in Kirov square them off and then cut the logs into square pieces roughly four inches by four inches—again, depending on the width of the blanks being produced. By contrast, as recently as 1995, workers at the Souvenir Factory in Sergiev Posad still split logs with an axe.

*Plate: 035*
*Factory: Art Alliance, Kirov*
*The lathe operator creates a series of matryoshka tops. He will create four or five tops from one log. Unlike most operators, he has created almost all of the outsides of the pieces before hollowing out the insides.*

## Turning the Blanks

Once the rounded or square block of wood has been processed, the logs, often after curing for another few weeks, go to the fine lathe operator. Unlike the preceding operations, the final turning process is a manual process, regardless of the size of the factory. Whether it be the small operations in Maidan or Sergiev Posad or the larger factories in Nolinsk, Semyonov, and Kirov, operators stand at lathes to form the doll. In Maidan, where almost all of the lathe operators are men, their fathers and grandfathers before them were woodworkers. Elsewhere, many of the lathe operators are women. Interestingly, most of the women who operate lathes learned their craft in the Soviet period. Now that democracy has arrived in Russia, women generally choose to paint, leaving the mechanical tasks to men.

The lathe operators use gouges—long-handled,

*Plate: 036*
*Factory: Vyatskii Souvenir, Nolinsk*
*Since the top of the blank is cut off the main piece of the wood using a gouge, the top often needs to be sanded by hand to make it smooth.*

curved chisels—to form the doll. They insert the round piece of wood into a spiked hub and beat it into place with a large mallet. The hub holds the wood tight, and the wood is rotated at the desired speed. On many of the elementary lathes, turning speed is adjusted by moving the belt that transfers torque from an electric motor to the turning axle from among several diameters of belt wheel, either on the motor's driveshaft or on the axle of the lathe, much like shifting gears on a multi-speed bicycle.

The operators direct the gouge to the middle of the piece that is to become the bottom half of the nesting doll, quickly hollowing out the rotating wood. Using a large, curved gouge, the operators remove most of the wood from the inside of the piece. Then they use a flat chisel to create the rabbeted edge that will form the seam with the top piece, making an angle that is just a little sharper than a right angle. This creates a slight pop when the top and bottom pieces are pressed together. The outside of the bottom piece is next. If it is the biggest of the pieces—the outermost piece of the doll—then it almost always has a notch near the bottom, creating a base. None of the inside pieces has a base, so those pieces are tapered from top to bottom. Finally, a sharp chisel is used to create a flat bottom and to separate it from the rest of the piece of wood. Several pieces are made from that one approximately two-foot

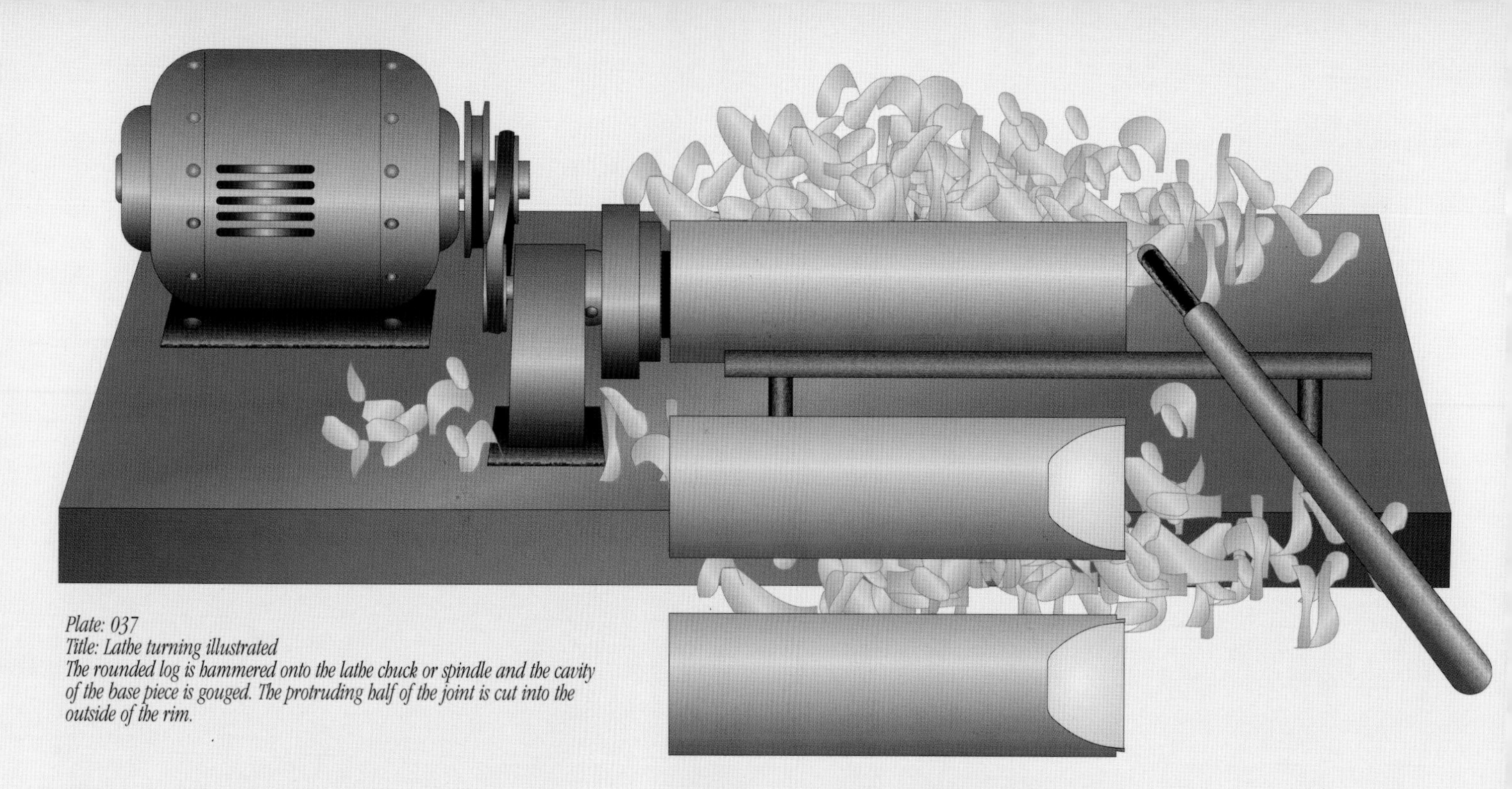

*Plate: 037*
*Title: Lathe turning illustrated*
*The rounded log is hammered onto the lathe chuck or spindle and the cavity of the base piece is gouged. The protruding half of the joint is cut into the outside of the rim.*

*The exterior of the bottom piece is cut. When fully shaped, it is separated from the log with a slightly concaved bottom to ensure stability when the doll sits on a flat surface. (While this diagram shows the turning of a single doll, bottom and top, typically, a batch of bottoms is turned at once, and then the tops are cut, each to fit a specific bottom piece.)*

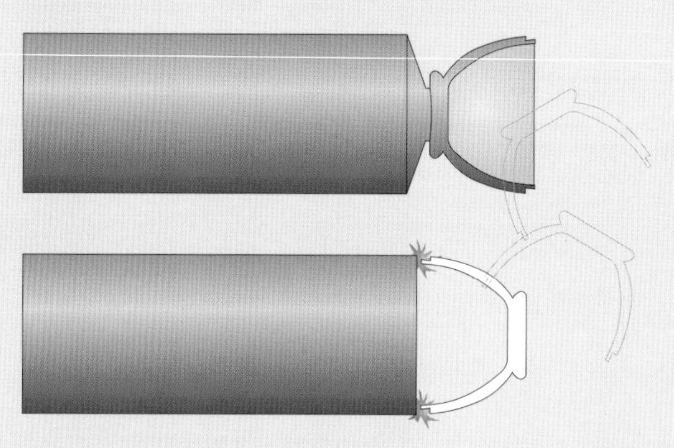

*The bottom opening is pressed onto the bottom face of the top piece, burning an edge guide for gouging the cavity and the exterior of the top.*

*The cavity of the top piece is gouged. The receding half of the joint is cut into the interior of the rim, also guided by the burn marks.*

*The bottom piece is inserted into the top piece to ensure a snug fit. Then the exterior form of the top piece is cut. While the top piece is still attached to the lathe, and the pieces are joined, they are trimmed together to make a smooth seam, and sometimes sanded.*

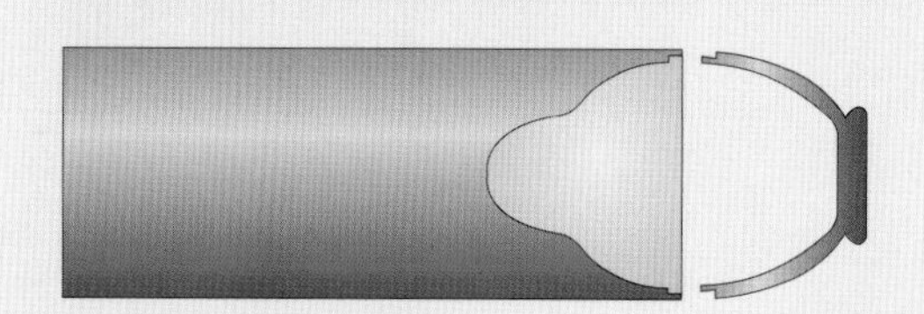

*Each progressively smaller doll is cut in the same way, usually without use of a template or pattern. The smaller, interior dolls are cut from smaller diameter logs.*

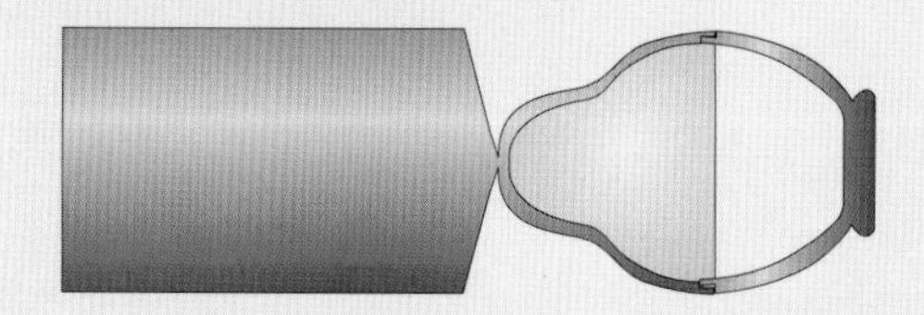

*Plate: 038 (top, left)*
*Factory: Semyonovskaya Rospis, Semyonov*
*The lathe operator uses a mallet to pound the log onto the chuck of the lathe.*

*Plate: 039 (top, right)*
*Factory: Semyonovskaya Rospis, Semyonov*
*Wood is removed from the interior of the bottom piece. A number of top pieces, sitting on the workbench, have already been made.*

*Plate: 040 (bottom, left)*
*Factory: Semyonovskaya Rospis, Semyonov*
*With the top piece fit into the bottom piece, the joint is smoothed while still on the lathe.*

*Plate: 041 (bottom, right)*
*Factory: Semyonovskaya Rospis, Semyonov*
*A pencil mark is made across the joint to show where top and bottom were joined on the lathe—the optimum fit—as a guide to the painters.*

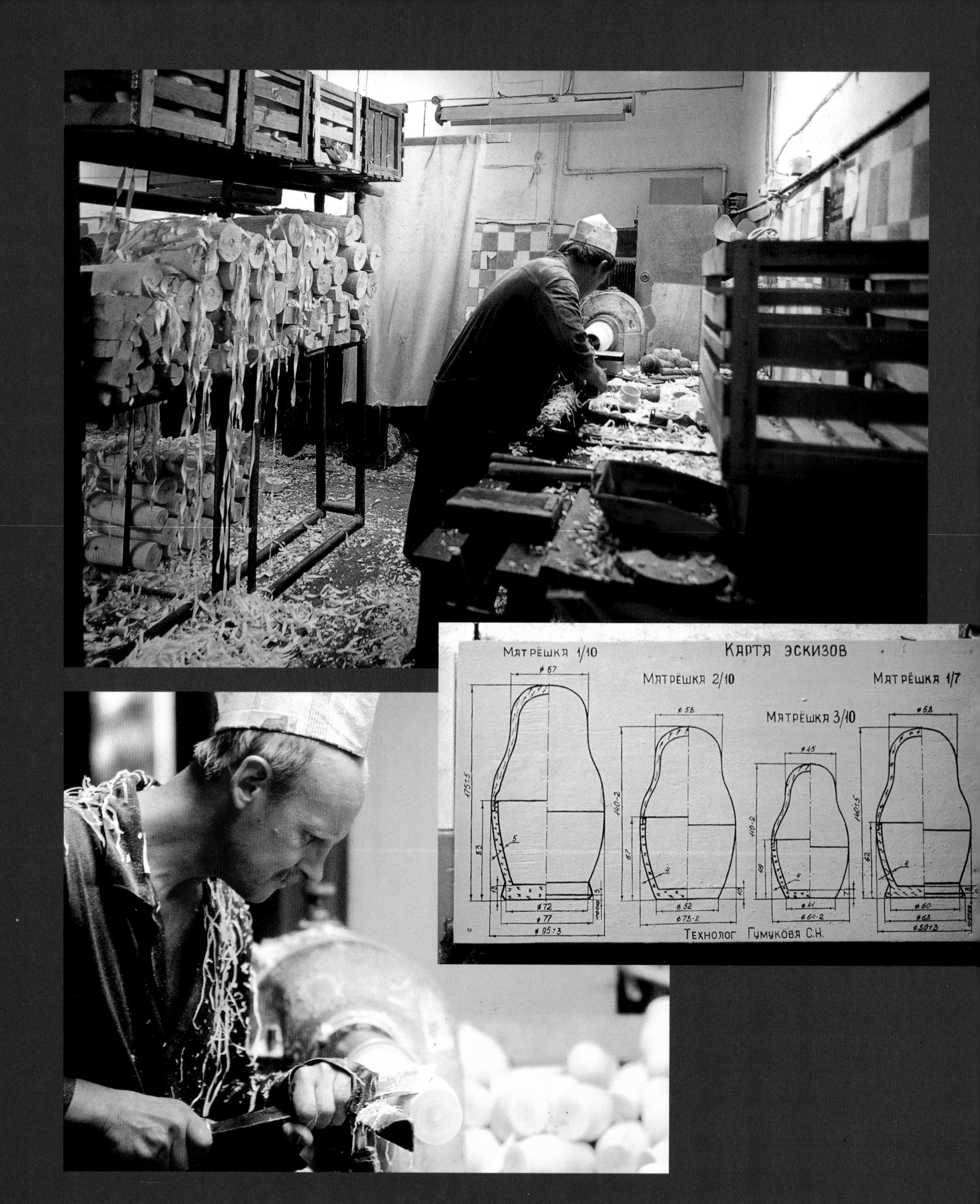
Карта эскизов
Матрёшка 1/10
Матрёшка 2/10
Матрёшка 3/10
Матрёшка 1/7
Технолог Гумукова С.Н.

*Plate: 042 (opposite page, top)*
*Factory: Vyatskii Souvenir, Nolinsk*
*A ready supply of logs is kept close to the lathe operator. Though shavings are strewn wildly from the turning, few factories have operating vacuum or even air filtration systems.*

*Plate: 043 (opposite page, middle)*
*Factory: Vyatskii Souvenir, Nolinsk*
*Though working drawings are done for new designs, once the design has been turned, the drawings are seldom used for reference. The skill of the lathe operator is more art than science. It is uncommon to see drawings in the shop.*

*Plate: 044 (opposite page, bottom)*
*Factory: Vyatskii Souvenir, Nolinsk*
*Headwear is used to keep sawdust and shavings out of the hair. It is often a real hat or, for women, a cloth bandanna. But it may also be a paper construction, made for the day or until it disintegrates from wear.*

*Plate: 045 (above)*
*Factory: AOFIS, Sergiev Posad*
*This woman has been operating a lathe for over 30 years. She produces precise, small nesting doll blanks using only her years of experience to assure a fit.*

*Plate: 046 (above)*
*Factory: Semyonovskaya Rospis, Semyonov*
*In Semyonov, the lathe operators are just as likely to be women as men.*

*Plate: 047 (right)*
*Factory: Art Alliance, Kirov*
*After blanks are made, they are packed in a crate, either for storage or to be taken directly to the painting rooms.*

length of wood mounted on the lathe.

Generally, lathe operators will spend a few hours making bottoms of one size, and then the next few hours making tops to fit the bottoms. Making the top is similar to making the bottom. Again, the operator beats the wood onto the hub and sets it into motion spinning the round piece of wood. In Maidan and most of the factories, the operator takes the bottom of the doll that was made earlier and holds it against the spinning wood. This creates friction, burning a circle in the bottom of the top workpiece and in the lip of the bottom piece of the doll. The burn marks are guides for cutting the opposing rabbeted joint and the cavity of the top piece. That is why most matryoshki, when opened, have a burned strip around the inside edge.

The only measurement tool that lathe operators commonly use is a simple caliper. This is a tool used for making sure that each piece is the same height. Operators use the "mouth" of the caliper to mark the starting point for the top. With no templates or patterns, they make the proper curve on the insides of the pieces so that the next, smaller doll will fit into it.

When the inside of the doll is finished, the lathe operators round off the top of the doll to conform to the curve on the inside. When the top is rounded, operators use the flat gouge to cut the piece off the mounted log. This process continues

*Plate: 048*
*Factory: Art Alliance, Kirov*
*The smallest pieces are made on an automatic lathe, often from birch wood. Birch is less expensive than linden, but harder, and therefore impractical to turn by hand. The automatic lathes are extremely loud, making ear protection very important.*

until all of the tops are made. Many lathe operators attach a finished bottom onto the top piece while it is on the lathe and run the chisel up and down the doll to ensure a smooth seam. Sometimes they use a piece of sandpaper to make the seam even smoother. Many operators make a pencil mark across the seam, indicating to the artist how to assemble the two pieces for the best fit. No doll, they say, is perfectly round, so it fits together best when the pencil marks are aligned.

*Plate: 049*
*Factory: Vyatskii Souvenir, Nolinsk*
*In Nolinsk, small blanks are again mounted on a machine and sanded by hand. The woman's fingers are taped to avoid abrasion.*

At some factories, the matryoshki are sent to a finishing lathe. If the blanks do not fit together perfectly, this last lathe operator puts the finishing touches on them to make sure that they do.

A finished nesting doll constitutes only about 20 percent of the log from which it is made. The rest of it becomes voluminous piles of shavings and sawdust on the lathe room floor. The shavings and sawdust constitute a fire hazard, especially in Russia, where a large percentage of the population smokes. Furthermore, breathing this fine wood dust cannot be good for the lungs. In Russia, though, matryoshka production is providing much needed jobs, and environmental concerns are secondary to employment.

In the course of a morning or evening, a lathe operator may make about fifty bottoms. Thus, an average operator makes fifty doll pieces (tops and bottoms) in a day and, therefore, fifty 5-piece blanks per week. Some of the best lathe operators can produce up to one hundred 5-piece blanks in a week.

There are only a few significant differences between small lathe operations in Maidan and Sergiev Posad compared to the large operations in the larger factories. One is the number of operators. In the smaller Sergiev Posad factories and, of course, Maidan, there are only one or two lathe operators. In the factories of Semyonov, Kirov, and Nolinsk, there are fifteen or twenty.

Another difference is the equipment. The Maidan backyard lathes are primarily built from parts, including a motor, pulley wheels, belts, and shafts. The tool rests, which must be adjusted depending on the diameter of the piece, are mounted on wood supports that pass through holes in the work bench. The support has a slot at the bottom through which a wedge tightens it against the bench. The wedge is hammered in to tighten or beaten out to loosen the support. Factories more commonly have industrial lathes.

Larger factories also have automatic lathes.

*Plate: 050-051 (above and right)*
*Factory: Khokhlomskaya Rospis, Semyonov*
*Blanks are brought to starching in large trays. After being starched, it is important that the blanks be placed so that their surfaces do not touch.*

*Plate: 052 (above)*
*Factory: Vyatskii Souvenir, Nolinsk*
*Starch is applied to the blanks by hands dipped into large bowls of heavy starch.*

*Plate: 053 (right)*
*City: Maidan*
*Size: 15-piece, 11 inches tall*
*The design on the Maidan doll is outlined in black, then painted with large stylized roses.*

These automatic lathes are used only to turn the inexpensive 3-piece or 4-piece birch wood dolls. They duplicate a pattern rapidly and consistently, producing several blanks a minute. Producers maintain, however, that the larger dolls must be made by hand, as the mechanical gouges of the automatic lathes would break a high percentage of the dolls, even if they were made from linden.

## Priming and Painting the Blanks

Now the blanks are ready to be painted. In Maidan, the next step is easy. While almost all adult males (and their teenage sons) in Maidan operate lathes in their backyards, almost all of their wives and daughters paint matryoshka dolls.

In factories, the blanks are put into trays and then carried to the starch

*Plate: 054 (above)*
*Factory: Semyonovskaya Rospis, Semyonov*
*The starch is made a day in advance of application and allowed to ferment slightly to speed absorbtion and drying. Dolls on the shelf in the background are designed to hold half-liter vodka bottles. They will be painted with military hats and brightly colored uniforms.*

*Plate: 055 (left)*
*Factory: Semyonovskaya Rospis, Semyonov*
*Typically, women perform the starching process. They dip their hands into the starch and roll pieces, small or large, in their palms to achieve even coatings on the blanks.*

*Plate: 056 (above, upper)*
*Factory: Vyatskii Souvenir, Nolinsk*
*The artists concentrate on their painting, but also chat. The eggs are personal purchases from a farmer who brings his goods to the factory.*

*Plate: 057 (above, lower)*
*Factory: Semyonovskaya Rospis, Semyonov*
*At Semyonovskaya Rospis, a few artists draw the outlines of the face, arms, etc., which are later filled in by other artists.*

room. Here they are rubbed with a liquid starch. The starch seals the wood so that aniline paint will apply flat and not blossom or bleed into unintended areas. When the blanks are ready to be painted, workers carry them on trays to the painting room. In large factories, these are large rooms, maybe seventy or eighty feet long, in which about a hundred artists work.

As late as 1994 in the Souvenir factory, artists painted one part of the doll and then passed the doll on to a colleague who painted another part. One painted the background colors of the doll, the next outlined the face and the apron, a third painted the face, a fourth the design on the apron, a fifth the flowers on the scarf, and a sixth put on the finishing

touches. The Souvenir artists took turns—the next day the woman who was painting scarves changed to painting faces to keep from getting bored. In Semyonov today, there are a few artists who just draw the outlines of the faces and aprons. They then turn the doll over to other artists who fill in the areas that have been outlined.

In the small Sergiev Posad factories, the rooms are smaller, and about ten artists sit and work. If the artists are painting traditional dolls, they generally have rows of dolls in front of them, arranged with the largest pieces at the back. They usually paint the background color first, on each of the 50 pieces. Then they might add the scarf, then the flowers, and so on. Usually, the face comes last,

*Plate: 058-059-060*
*Factory: Khokhlomskaya Rospis, Semyonov*
*The curls on these dolls are sometimes applied to cover blemishes in the wood. The black paint for the curls is applied with a cloth that is folded and rolled in a tight spiral. The pattern of these curls stamped on the dolls is typically irregular, to suit the artist's whim.*

although artists say that the order in which they paint depends upon their mood. If they are painting a more individual artistic doll, they would paint one doll at a time, although they would paint all of the pieces with the background color before applying the more artistic touches on each piece.

A design motif used in several factories is the pinwheel-shaped spiral. It is achieved by rolling folded cloth tightly, then dipping it in paint and applying it, rubber-stamp fashion, onto the heads or other parts of the dolls. Often, real rouge makeup is used for the rosy cheeks on the dolls. Other techniques are explained in Chapter 3.

*Plate: 061*
*Factory: AOFIS, Sergiev Posad*
*Removing lacquer from the hands at the end of the day is done (by some) with diesel fuel. Of all the lacquerers who were interviewed, not one spoke of dermatological problems.*

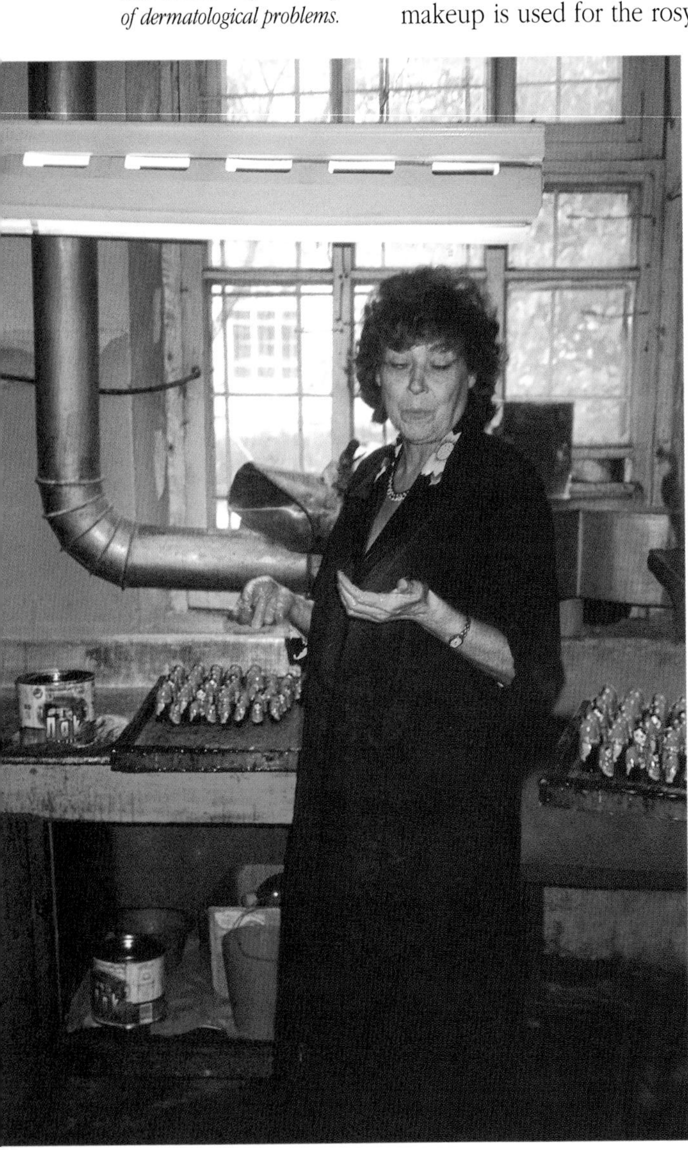

## Lacquering the Dolls

Once the doll is painted, it is taken to the lacquer rooms. Even the largest factories have only a few lacquerers. The small Sergiev Posad factories have only one lacquerer, and even they do not always stay busy. Most lacquer rooms consist of a series of shelves, reminiscent of a commercial bakery. The lacquer person, who seems always to be a woman, takes a painted matryoshka piece (one of a set) from one shelf, dips her hand in the lacquer, and rolls the piece back and forth between her hands, just as a child might make a snake out of modeling clay, and then places it on the drying shelf.

The women who lacquer dolls are unconcerned about the effect the lacquer has on their hands or health. Asked how the lacquer is cleaned from her hands at the end of the day, one woman replied, "With diesel fuel—it makes my hands soft." The woman who lacquers the dolls at Factory No.1 uses sunflower oil to wash off the bulk of the lacquer, and then "a special solvent" to get her hands clean.

The lacquer dries for twenty-four hours; then the process is repeated. Most factories apply two or three layers of lacquer. The layers of lacquer need to be thin, in order to avoid ugly accumulations of lacquer that sometimes occur at the seam on the top piece and at the top of the base on the bottom piece.

On fine art nesting dolls, lacquer is generally applied with a brush, which is less likely to show flaws. A good brush lacquerer, however, can only do about ten 5-piece dolls per week, whereas a bare-handed lacquerer can easily do up to ten times that many. Either way, a good lacquerer using glossy lacquer produces such a shiny exterior that some people mistake it for porcelain. Would an automated process produce the same effect? Charmingly, no one seems to have tried to find out.

*Plate: 062 (above, top)*
*Factory: AOFIS, Sergiev Posad*
*Certainly the most surprising procedure of all is the application of lacquer. "By hand" has a very literal meaning.*

*Plate: 063-064 (above and left)*
*Factory: Semyonovskaya Rospis, Semyonov*
*The lacquer pot is well used. Three coats of lacquer on each doll is usual for most dolls. Shown here are the traditional yellow Semyonov nesting dolls.*

*Plate: 065 (above)*
*Factory: Vyatskii Souvenir, Nolinsk*
*These bottle holders are finished and ready to be sold.*

*Plate: 066 (left)*
*Factory: Art Alliance, Kirov*
*After the dolls are painted, lacquered, and dried, they must be taken apart, breaking the lacquer coating over the joint. These women pop open each piece, and then insert the smaller pieces inside as they assemble each complete doll.*

# Classifying Matryoshki

# Every Face an Eyelash Different

## Classifying Matryoshki

# Every Face an Eyelash Different

*Plate: 067 (chapter title)*
*Title: Girls in Flowers*
*Artist: Ye. Fabianskaya*
*Size: 7-piece, 7 inches tall*

*Plate: 068 (opposite)*
*City: Sergiev Posad*
*Artist: Ira Z.*
*Size: 30-piece, 17 inches tall*

ALTHOUGH THE HANDCRAFTED nature of matryoshka production has barely changed over the years, the variety of dolls has mushroomed. Therefore, this chapter discusses the various characteristics that can be used to classify matryoshki and to make sense of their seemingly infinite differences. The chapter begins with the basic features common to matryoshka dolls and then discusses the following characteristics: number of pieces, size, shape, paint and technique, pattern and color, and type, including accessories based upon matryoshka dolls.

Matryoshki share several basic characteristics:

- Typical dolls have a face at the top. The middle of the doll is the stomach.
- Most have a shawl surrounding their head.
- Almost all matryoshki have a spot of red on their cheeks, representing rosy or rouged cheeks.
- Some of the finest dolls have a medallion: a round section, usually black, painted on the stomach.
- Traditional matryoshki have aprons; most nontraditional ones do not.
- Almost all outside dolls—and almost no inside dolls—have a base, where the wood flares out to create a stable bottom.
- Most, but not all, have eyelashes.

## The Number of Pieces

The most important characteristic used in classifying nesting dolls is the number of pieces. The Russian word for a nesting doll piece is *mesto,* so a marking of 5 m or 10 m written on the bottom of a matryoshka indicates that it has 5 or 10 pieces, respectively.

Although some matryoshki consist of only one piece, the smallest number of pieces is generally three. Five-piece dolls have become the industry standard and account for approximately half of all nesting dolls. The one notable exception is the standard Semyonov doll, which has six pieces. This is the doll that was chosen for *The Littlest Matryoshka,* a popular children's book by Corinne Demas Bliss.

Since the demise of the Soviet Union and the advent of market demand, the most common sizes made beyond the standard 5-piece are 7-piece, 10-piece, and 15-piece. Any doll with more than twenty pieces is quite expensive. Thirty-piece

*Plate: 069 (above)*
*Title: Minimat*
*City: Sergiev Posad*
*Size: 5-piece, 3.5 inches tall*
*A group of Sergiev Posad artists paints hundreds of these little minimats every month.*

*Plate: 070 (opposite)*
*(top)*
*Title: Grigorieva Minimat*
*City: Sergiev Posad*
*Artist: N. Grigorieva*
*Size: 5-piece, 4 inches tall*
*Natasha Grigorieva's cute faces and vibrant use of colors grace these little 5-piece dolls.*
*(middle)*
*Title: Micro Snowman 10-piece*
*City: Sergiev Posad*
*Artist: Valery Aleksandrovsky*
*Size: 10-piece, 1.7 inches tall*
*It is hard to believe that there can be 10 pieces to this tiny doll. The smallest piece is the smallest made – about the size of a small grain of sand.*
*(bottom)*
*Title: Micro Girl with Teddy Bear*
*City: Sergiev Posad*
*Size: 5-piece, 1.5 inches tall*
*All but the innermost piece of this tiny doll have teddy bears on their stomachs.*

dolls have become the standard of the high end, but occasionally lathe operators create 40- and 50-piece dolls. The largest finished doll on record is 72 pieces, made in a Semyonov factory. A lathe operator in Maidan is known to have produced a 75-piece matryoshka blank, but it had not been painted as of this writing.

## The Size of a Doll

Generally, large nesting dolls are more expensive than small ones. While this may seem obvious, it is sometimes a point of confusion. It seems that artists (and often, buyers) place inordinate importance on the size of a doll. Following market practice, stores in the U.S. typically charge more for a 6-inch, 5-piece nesting doll than for a 5-inch, 5-piece doll. Yet it does not take much more work to paint the slightly larger doll. More logically, a very small matryoshka is more expensive than a larger doll because of the ability needed to paint such tiny surfaces.

For purposes of classification, TolsToys has developed names for the different sizes. We often refer to matryoshki as "mats." Small dolls that are only three to four inches tall are minimats, and very small ones are micromats. Most factory dolls are full-sized matryoshki. Sizes vary according to city—the Semyonov 6-piece is only about five inches tall, whereas Sergiev Posad and Maidan 5-piece dolls are usually about six inches tall.

Most minimats are alike throughout. Those that do have variations are generally a little more expensive than standard minimats. They come in both standard and potbelly shapes (see "Shape" below) and often are the first pieces in a child's collection. Most minimats are made by individuals, but they are also produced in the factories in Kirov and Nolinsk.

One of the most fascinating developments in nesting doll production is the micromat. As with

*Plate: 071 (above)*
*City: Sergiev Posad*
*Artist: N. Grigorieva*
*Size: 10-piece, 5 inches tall*
*Natasha Grigorieva paints wonderful faces and uses unusual colors ranging from pink to black. This doll illustrates how a pot-bellied doll can accommodate a large number of pieces.*

*Plate: 072 (left)*
*Title: Minimat, Platok*
*City: Sergiev Posad*
*Size: 5-piece, 4 inches tall*
*Another small doll, named for its colorful scarf (*platok *is the Russian word for scarf).*

the standard dolls, the most common micromats have five pieces. But, since they are typically only about 1.25 inches high, the smallest piece is about the size of a grain of rice. And these are the medium-sized ones. Micromats are so small that it is hard to believe that the smallest pieces are actually turned. Valery Aleksandrovsky, of Sergiev Posad, produces perhaps the most popular micromat, a 10-piece snowman, who, with his top hat, stands about 1.75 inches high. The smallest piece in this doll is so tiny that, if it is dropped on a carpet, it is almost impossible to find. Admittedly, the last piece does not have much painting on it, usually two or three dots, but its size alone is amazing.

Aleksei Kremnev paints micromats in his apartment. Like factory painters, he paints several dolls at a time and lines them up on a table. However, rather than sitting on a high stool, he sits on a couch, and the coffee table is his table. Each piece rests on a clever looking holder. It is not a specially designed holder, but rather the disposable needle from a syringe. The pieces are so minute that an artist could not possibly hold them in his hand, so Aleksei simply sticks them on the needle and holds onto the plastic end of the needle.

## Matryoshka Shapes

Most nesting dolls are shaped somewhat like the upper part of the human body, with the arms held close to the body. The dolls of Sergiev Posad and Maidan tend to be a little wider in the stomach than those of Semyonov, which are a little taller and thinner.

New shapes appear constantly. Ironically, photos of early twentieth-century dolls show that some of the earliest dolls were also unusually shaped. But Soviet standardization largely eliminated shape variation in the 1930s. Among the earliest matryoshki were rounded cones and some that were almost bottle-shaped. The rounded cones have reappeared. The new ones open near the bottom, giving them a bell-shaped look. Also reappearing, but still unusual, are cones with pointed tops. Conical dolls are usually 3-piece and, for some reason, often depict Santas.

Several lathe operators and artists have revived another traditional symbolic shape: the egg. Eggs on stands, or with strings so that they can be hung, are a popular item in Russia. Russian women have traditionally worn small eggs around their necks at Easter time. As was mentioned, wooden eggs were made in the late nineteenth century by the same lathe operators who would later produce nesting dolls. Probably because of the association of eggs with Easter, egg-shaped matryoshki often depict religious scenes or Orthodox icons. Strictly speaking, reproducing icons is considered sacrilegious, but these items are quite popular.

Recently, other shapes have appeared. One that has become relatively common is what we call the "potbelly." These are dolls that are almost as wide as they are tall. Potbellies have two

*Plate: 073 (above)*
*Title: Micro Girl 3-piece*
*City: Sergiev Posad*
*Artist: L. and A. Kremnev*
*Size: 3-piece, 0.8 inches tall*
*Even the outside doll of a 3-piece micromat is tiny. This doll is shown in actual size.*

*Plate: 074 (overleaf)*
*City: Sergiev Posad*
*Artist: Unknown*
*Size: 30-piece, 6.5 inches tall*
*The ultimate illustration of the use of the pot-bellied shape to get a large number of dolls into a small space. The walls of the middle pieces of this doll are paper-thin.*

BOSS
Africa
Egypt
Japan
N.America

disadvantages: because of their round shape, they are a little harder to grasp and therefore to open, and their round shape makes them more likely to stick inside the next larger doll. They do, however, have one big advantage: their shape gives room for more dolls. The most common potbelly, which is only about five inches tall and four inches wide, is a 10-piece. By comparison, the most common 10-piece doll from Maidan, Semyonov, or Kirov, is usually three inches taller.

One of the more impressive high end dolls is a potbelly doll that is only about seven inches tall and contains 30 pieces. However, even though the potbelly shape lends itself to more dolls, the 30-piece dolls have incredibly thin walls. The walls of some of the inner dolls are so thin that black paint used on the outside of the doll can seep through the wood to the inside.

Viktor Nikitin from Dubna, a small city just west of Sergiev Posad, has formed a group that makes spherical matryoshki. These matryoshki originated as globes, with the continents represented on the outside. Some of these globes still have short bases, similar to those of matryoshki, but most now have three-inch-tall bases, similar to egg stands but attached to the globe. The inside contains 14 or 15 wooden figures, not nested, representing peoples of the world.

The Dubna group now makes globes with animals of the world, circuses, and a nativity scene.

*Plate: 075 (opposite, top)*
*Title: Mother and Children*
*Factory: Art Alliance, Kirov*
*Artist: Factory artists*
*Size: 5-piece, 5 inches tall*
*A variation on the grandmother doll, this mother with children is an unusual product of the Kirov factory.*

*Plate: 076, 077 (opposite, bottom)*
*Title: People of the World*
*City: Dubna*
*Artist: T. Gladkova*
*Size: 15-piece, 8 inches tall (including stand)*
*The globe opens to reveal people from around the world. The nationalities are written on the bottom of each piece (sometimes in Russian, sometimes English). The base of the boy with "BOSS" on his shirt, lying between Egypt and Japan, reads "Teenager."*

*Plate: 078 (above)*
*Title: Life of Christ*
*City: Raduzhnoye*
*Artist: N. Pugaeva*
*Size: 5-piece, 6 inches tall*
*Collection: Vicki Miller*
*This is one of many egg-shaped nesting dolls that has religious themes.*

*Plate: 079 (left)*
*Title: Rounded Cone*
*City: Sergiev Posad*
*Size: 5-piece, 4 inches tall*

They also produce a smaller spherical doll, about four inches in diameter, with a small base, portraying such subjects as a circus, snow play, and minstrels. Inside these smaller globes are four small people or animals.

Vera Andreyeva of Sergiev Posad paints a large, hollow wooden turnip with three dolls inside representing the first three characters of the traditional Russian tale of *The Turnip*. Each one of these three dolls—the grandfather, grandmother, and granddaughter—has one doll inside representing the dog, cat, and mouse of the story. (For a short description of these folk tales, see Chapter 4.) Similarly, Andreyeva does a *Kolobok* (*The Roll*), a Russian version of *The Gingerbread Man,* which is round like a roll, with its traditional figures—an old lady, an old man, and a bear, inside of which are a rabbit, a fox, a wolf, and a roll.

Recently, Vera Andreyeva and other artists have been painting nesting spheres and mushrooms.

*Plate: 081 (opposite)*
*(top, left)*
*Title: Russian Costumes*
*Artist: Irina Zorina*
*Size: 5-piece, 6 inches tall*
*Collection: Jo Kessel Buyske*
*The artist uses the cone shape to represent dresses from various regions of Russia.*
*(bottom, left)*
*Baba Yaga*
*City: Sergiev Posad*
*Artist: A. Yevteyev*
*Size: 4-piece, 5 inches tall*
*Baba Yaga is sitting on the bucket that transports her and her broom. The doll illustrates a part of* The Frog Princess, *in which Baba Yaga helps Ivan Tsarevich track down his beloved Vasilisa. Vasilisa is being held prisoner by the evil Koshchei the Immortal, an enemy of Baba Yaga. Baba Yaga tells Ivan that he must cross the sea to an island, uproot the oak tree, free the duck, and break the duck's egg. Inside the egg he will find a needle, and when he breaks the needle, Koshchei will die and Ivan can go to Vasilisa. This doll consists of Baba Yaga, warts and all; her traditional house on a chicken leg (the roof comes off); the egg; and the needle.*

*(top, right)*
*Title: Snow Queen*
*City: Sergiev Posad*
*Artist: A. Yevteyev*
*Size: 4-piece, 5 inches tall*
*Hans Christian Andersen's story of the Snow Queen comes alive here as the beautiful but evil Snow Queen opens to reveal Gerda and her friend, and then finally a small snowman.*
*(bottom, right)*
*Title: Kolobok Bear*
*City: Sergiev Posad*
*Artist: A. Yevteyev*
*Size: 3-piece, 5.5 inches tall*
*The bread rolls past this bear as it runs away from the old couple. It is hard to tell that the doll nests, as the bear has a snout, ears, and feet. The second piece, the fox, also has a long nose. The inside piece is the roll, complete with feet.*

*Plate: 082 (above)*
*Title: The Turnip*
*City: Orekhovo-Zuyevo*
*Artist: S. Koblov*
*Size: 7-piece, 7 inches tall*
*One of the finest dolls depicting the story of* The Turnip, *highlighted by the little carved turnip in the middle.*

*Plate: 082*
*Title: The Polar Express*
*City: St. Petersburg*
*Artist: I. Yu. Bobkova*
*Size: 7-piece, 7 inches tall*
*Based on the perennial favorite children's Christmas book by Chris Van Allsburg, this matryoshka is produced by TolsToys under license from publisher Houghton Mifflin Co.*

Unlike most matryoshki, each of the five pieces in the spherical dolls has a base. The mushrooms are shaped just like mushrooms; the base is slightly flared, and the top of the mushroom is rabbeted so that it fits over the bottom of the doll. Each of the pieces inside is also mushroom shaped.

Other unusual nesting doll shapes are created by gluing carved and turned shapes. The inside dolls of the Andreyeva turnip and *kolobok* are made in that manner. Another artist, Aleksandr Evteyev, has copied a doll in the shape of the famous Russian witch, Baba Yaga, complete with a long nose and extensive warts, not to mention the trademark broom and upside-down bucket on which she flies. Inside the Baba Yaga is a house on a chicken leg (the traditional home of Baba Yaga). The roof of the house opens to reveal an egg, which in turn contains a needle, both items being a part of a folk tale involving Baba Yaga's evil enemy, Koshchei the Immortal.

The same artist makes a similar doll depicting a bear complete with head and paws in the

*Plate: 083 (left)*
*Title: The Scribe*
*City: Sergiev Posad*
*Artist: N.D. Bartram*
*Size: 3-piece, 6 inches*
*Collection: Museum of Applied Folk Art*
*This bullet-shaped doll, common in Ukraine, was painted in the 1910s. This shape has become rare.*

*Plate: 084 (below)*
*Country: Ukraine*
*Size: 4.5 inches, 5-piece*
*Collection: Gail Buyske*
*This doll has the shape common in Russia, but colorfully illustrates traditional Ukrainian costumes.*

story of *The Roll*. Inside the bear is a fox, and then a cute little roll, complete with shoes that, presumably, enable the roll to run faster. Evteyev also makes a *Snow Queen* with a large collar and a long, flowing skirt. Inside the Snow Queen are a little boy, a little girl, and a snowman.

The smallest piece of a matryoshka can be any shape, as it does not have to hold another piece. Sergei Koblov, an artist who carves designs into the matryoshki, makes a beautiful turnip doll featuring a small, realistic-looking turnip as the innermost piece. Several lathe operators make a round bread roll for the smallest piece of the *Kolobok*. TolsToys produces a doll based on the popular children's Christmas book, *The Polar Express*, in which the innermost piece is a jingle bell.

In this period when new shapes are constantly appearing, an old, more traditional shape has

*Plate: 085*
*Title: The Golden Ring*
*City: Sergiev Posad*
*Artist: Sv. Medvedeva*
*Size: 10-piece, 5 inches tall*
*Sveta Medvedeva's wood burned depictions of the cathedrals and monasteries on the Golden Ring are combined with an unusual white scarf that brings out the illustration. She writes the names of the cities on the first five dolls.*

*Plate: 086 (right)*
*Title: Musicians*
*City: Orekhovo-Zuyevo*
*Artist: S. Koblov*
*Size: 5-piece, 6.5 inches tall*
*This example of Sergei Koblov's carved matryoshka presents a theme often seen: a family of musicians.*

*Plate: 087 (above, left)*
*City: Sergiev Posad*
*Artist: Ira Z.*
*Size: 30-piece, 17 inches tall*
*A beautiful example of wood burning, with elaborate fairy tale illustrations on each piece.*

*Plate: 088 (above, right)*
*Title: Silver and Gold*
*City: Sergiev Posad*
*Artist: Unknown*
*Size: 5-piece, 4 inches tall*
*This bright doll features the use of wood burning as well as* potal, *which is foil ironed onto the doll to give the effect of gold or silver leaf.*

almost disappeared. The bullet-shaped matryoshka, which was simply a cylinder rounded at the top, has become rare. This shape was often associated with Ukraine, and it may be vanishing completely as production in that former Soviet republic decreases.

## Paint and Technique

Factories have traditionally used gouache or aniline paints. These are opaque and generally cover up discolorations or minor defects in the wood. Not surprisingly, as independent artists create new and different shapes, they also use more varied types of paints. Some use transparent watercolor paints, allowing the grain of the wood to show through the paint. This requires a high quality blank. Matte finishes are becoming more common, with either a matte lacquer or no lacquer at all. Unlacquered dolls are usually done with tempera or acrylic paints. Sergei Koblov, an artist featured in Chapter 6, is proud of his vegetable-based dyes, which provide rich color to emphasize, but not overpower, his carvings. He carefully guards the secret of the ingredients he uses in his dyes.

The technique of wood burning was common in the earliest matryoshka dolls but was rarely used in the Soviet factories. Today, some of the finest matryoshki are wood burned, or use a combination of wood burning and paint. Tamara Ruzakova's daisy doll combines tempera daisies with extensive wood burning. One style of nesting dolls features

*Plate: 089 (opposite)*
*Title: Red and Black Classical*
*Artist: TolsToys staff artist*
*Size: 5-piece, 6 inches tall*
*A typical classical doll, featuring a scarf covered with simple flowers, and a black base.*

*Plate: 090 (left, foreground)*
*Title: Gold Frame Classical*
*City: Sergiev Posad*
*Artist: Unknown*
*Size: 5-piece, 6 inches tall*
Potal *is used to outline many of the features of this doll. The two-toned blue would never have been used on a traditional doll.*

*Plate: 091 (left, background)*
*Artist: Unknown*
*Size: 15-piece, 11 inches tall*
*Collection: Vicki Miller*
*The best artists show as much attention to detail on the backs of the matryoshki as they do on the fronts. Note that the dark, textured background here is produced by wood burning.*

a back that is entirely wood burned, creating ridges that give the effect of a fancy overcoat.

A technique often seen on more expensive dolls is *potal* (pronounced po-TALL). This is the gold or silver sheen used to highlight the medallion or the face, or to add sheen to the design on a doll. Similar to gold leaf, *potal* is a heavier foil, like aluminum foil, that is applied to the wood using a hot iron or block. Artists rarely use gold leaf on nesting dolls, except as a base for painting done in the finest miniatures, much like the technique used in making Russian lacquer boxes.

Not all special techniques are used just for expensive dolls. One decorative technique used on relatively inexpensive dolls is the application of rye straw, dyed to different colors, dried, splayed and cut by hand

*Plate: 092*
*Title: Matryoshka with Straw*
*Factory: Vyatskii Souvenir, Nolinsk*
*Artist: factory artists*
*Flowers and designs in Nolinsk and Kirov are made with straw.*

into tiny shapes, and meticulously glued in place. This process is shown in Chapter 5 in the discussion about the factories of Kirov and Nolinsk.

## Pattern and Color

TolsToys refers to factory dolls or dolls done in the style of factory dolls as "traditional" matryoshki. Many traditional dolls are now made in private homes, however. For example, since the factory in Maidan ceased operation in the 1970s, all of the Maidan dolls are now painted in the artists' homes. In addition, there are many artists who paint in the traditional style in Sergiev Posad and elsewhere.

Traditional dolls are quite plain. All have scarves with flowers; most have aprons. Their eyes are usually black, and their cheeks are usually solid, round circles of pink. Traditional dolls are almost always alike from largest to smallest, with occasional exceptions such as a boy-and-girl doll.

Although all of the traditional factory dolls share characteristics, a nesting doll aficionado can look at a traditional matryoshka and identify its origin. For example, Sergiev Posad dolls have a distinct apron and their flowers are not outlined in black. They often carry a basket or some other object. Semyonov dolls traditionally have a yellow scarf and a red base, with one or more outlined roses on the stomach. The flowers are more realistic than those on a Maidan doll and the painting is more detailed. Maidan dolls are the most primitive and have the most vivid colors, such as pink, red, blue, orange, and yellow. Kirov and Nolinsk are in the same geographic area, so their dolls are quite similar. They resemble dolls from Semyonov, but their colors are much more varied, and they do not use outlining around their flowers.

We use the term "classical" to refer to a six-inch, 5-piece matryoshka, although the term also describes a nontraditional, but not very finely painted, doll. Perhaps the most striking difference between the classical and traditional matryoshka is the color. Traditional dolls are usually painted with bright or primary colors, especially blue, yellow, red, orange, and pink. Classical dolls make liberal use of black, which is only used to outline features of traditional dolls. In addition, forest green, navy blue, burgundy, violet, and deep red grace the scarves and bases of classical dolls.

*Plate: 092 (opposite)*
*Factory: Vyatskii Souvenir, Nolinsk*
*Artist: factory artists*
*Size: 12-piece, 10 inches tall*
*A large Nolinsk doll without the straw appliqué for which the factory is known.*

*Plate: 093 (below)*
*Collection: Gail Buyske*
*Lacquer boxes from Fedoskino (above) and Palekh (below) are readily recognized by their painting style. Both illustrate the* troika, *or three-horse sleigh.*

Classical patterns are varied, but they usually feature flowers rather than aprons, and often lack arms and hands. Their faces are not as standardized as traditional dolls. Their eyes tend to be more expressive than factory-painted eyes, and the rouge on their cheeks is more subtle.

Classicals sometimes feature medallions on their stomachs, on which flowers or landscapes are painted. More often, the flowers are painted on a shawl that is draped over the head of the doll and continues to the

*Plate: 094 (left)*
*Title: Black Classical*
*City: St. Petersburg*
*Artist: TolsToys staff artist*
*Size: 5-piece, 6 inches tall*
*These dolls represent the new standard for inexpensive nesting dolls. Unlike traditional dolls, they often do not have aprons or sleeves. Color is perhaps the biggest difference between traditional dolls and these new ones.*

*Plate: 095 (above)*
*Title: White Landscape Classical*
*City: Sergiev Posad*
*Size: 5-piece, 5 inches tall*
*Some contemporary matryoshki have medallions with simple but attractive miniatures on them. This doll has a white background to accentuate the winter scene on the medallion.*

*Plate: 096*
*Title: Gzhel Classical*
*City: St. Petersburg*
*Artist: TolsToys staff artist*
*Size: 5-piece, 6 inches tall*
*The blue and white of this doll is a reflection of the style of the traditional Russian porcelain called* Gzhel, *for the village in which it made.* Gzhel *is reminiscent of Delft ceramics.*

front of the doll. Flowered classicals are usually the same color and pattern as they get smaller. But other classicals depict a variety of objects held in the arms of the doll. One common theme is a series of musical instruments, another a series of vegetables, and a third depicts a samovar on the outside doll, followed by a teapot and other objects associated with teatime.

Matryoshki that cannot be classified as either traditional or classical are typically more complex and combine the characteristics described above in various ways. One good example is provided by matryoshki with medallions on their stomachs. The medallions portray a variety of scenes, including those from Russian fairy tales. Some of the finest matryoshka dolls have medallions on which are painted miniatures that rival the well known lacquer boxes made in the villages of Palekh, Fedoskino, Mstyora, and Kholui. In fact, matryoshka artists often copy scenes from lacquer boxes.

*Plate: 097(opposite)*
*Title: Braid Classical*
*City: Sergiev Posad*
*Size: 5-piece, 6 inches tall*
*Pinks, blues, and greens combine with a translucent paint to create a contemporary look. These simple, traditional designs exemplify the charm of the dolls.*

*Plate: 098*
*Title: Watercolor Classical*
*City: St. Petersburg*
*Artist: TolsToys staff artist*
*Size: 5-piece, 6 inches tall*
*This doll combines opaque and translucent paints of the same color, decorated with a few pink flowers.*

*Plate: 100 (above)*
*(background , left)*
*Title: Little Red Riding Hood*
*Factory: Semyonovskaya Rospis, Semyonov*
*Size: 1-piece, 5 inches tall*
*Little Red Riding Hood is as popular in Russia as it is in other countries. Here it appears on a* nevalyashka.

*(background, right)*
*Title: Grandfather Frost*
*Factory: Semyonovskaya Rospis, Semyonov*
*Size: 1-piece, 5 inches tall*
*Santas are a frequent theme on* nevalyashki.
*(foreground)*
*The inside of a* nevalyashka. *Note the weight in the bottom, with wires protruding upwards. One of the wires holds a clapper (in this case, a one-ruble coin), which creates a ringing sound when it strikes the other wires.*

*Plate: 101 (right)*
*Title: In a Meadow*
*Size: 1-piece, 5 inches tall*
*This* nevalyashka *was purchased in a kiosk at Yasnaya Polyana, Leo Tolstoy's estate south of Tula. The painting is well done, and the head unusual. Unfortunately, there is neither a signature nor an indication of where the doll is from.*

*Plate: 101*
*(background, center)*
*Title: Woman with Dogs*
*City: Dubna*
*Artist: Ilyicheva*
*Size: 13-piece, 7 inches tall*
*(continued below)*

*Plate: 101 (continued)*
*(foreground, left)*
*Title: Piggies*
*City: Dubna*
*Artist: Nikiforova*
*Size: 5-piece, 3 inches tall*
*This is a variation on the grandmother dolls produced by the Dubna group.*
*(foreground, right)*
*Title: Korobeinik*
*Artist: Matryona staff artist*
*Size: 8-piece, 8.5 inches tall*
*A Christmas doll filled with ornaments that can be hung by the strings.*
*(background, left)*
*Title: Snowballs*
*City: Dubna*
*Artist: T. Gladkova*
*Size: 5-piece, 4 inches tall*
*Viktor Nikitin and his group from Dubna specialize in spheres with small figures inside.*

These boxes, made exclusively in those four villages until recently, have a tradition longer than matryoshka dolls. They are exquisite works of art and can command very high prices.

## Types of Dolls

Other than the standard nesting doll, two types of matryoshki have been produced for many years, though they are still quite unusual: *nevalyashki* and *babushki*. The *nevalyashka* is not technically a nesting doll. Most people refer to it as a bell. The root of the word is *valyat'*, which means "to roll." The prefix *ne* means "not." So a *nevalyashka* is a doll that does not roll over. This doll is rounded on the bottom and weighted, so that it pops back up if you try to knock it over. Since the Russian word is untranslatable and difficult to pronounce, English speakers use a variety of terms to describe it: bell, musical, roly-poly, or even weeble.

For many years, I thought that these were simple dolls with a jingle bell inside and a weight

in the bottom. But when one of them broke, my son took it apart, revealing an elaborate construction. The weight is a disk, perhaps a quarter of an inch thick and an inch in diameter, and it is imbedded into the wood. Six to eight stiff wires that are soldered to and extend from the weight form the bell mechanism, and another wire holds a different disk the size of a small coin (in many cases, it actually is a coin), which acts as a clapper. If the weight comes loose, or if the clapper is hung too close to the weight, then the sound becomes a dull thud or a scraping noise. Looking at a *nevalyashka,* it is hard to believe that it costs about the same as a 5-piece nesting doll. But the mechanism certainly accounts for a large part of the cost. Most *nevalyashki* are painted quite simply and are very affordable. Like nesting dolls, however, elaborate *nevalyashki* are sought-after collectors' items and can sell for almost as much as an artistic nesting doll.

A second type of unusual doll is the *babushka,* or grandmother. In this variation of the matryoshka, the largest doll, the grandmother, opens up to reveal three smaller non-nested dolls, the daughters, inside. Each of these three dolls opens again, with three more little non-nested dolls, the granddaughters, inside each one. These also vary in complexity, but even the most simply painted grandmother costs about as much as a medium-priced standard nesting doll—it is, after all, a 13-piece doll.

Artist Viktor Nikitin, who works with his wife, daughter, and a group of artists in Dubna, makes grandmothers that depict a woman on the outside holding a cat, and then girls inside, and finally nine little cats with little cardboard ears. They also make small minimats that do not nest but have four small pieces inside.

Many variations on these types of matryoshki have appeared. The globe, sphere, and mushroom dolls have already been described. A group of artists that calls itself Matryona has developed a doll shaped like a traditional matryoshka, but instead of other nested dolls, inside it are tall, thin Christmas ornaments—people, soldiers, and even churches. This is called a *korobeinik,* a nineteenth-century word meaning "peddler." These dolls were given the name because they are reminiscent of the sample case that the peddler carried. A large *korobeinik* consists of a standard looking eight-inch-tall matryoshka as an outer shell, with eight or nine ornaments inside. Smaller *korobeiniki* are only about four inches tall, and their ornaments often lack hooks.

One other type of nesting doll is the bottle holder. This doll consists of only one piece. It is turned to accommodate a bottle, usually a half-liter (one pint) vodka bottle, but it also holds *champanskaya,* Russia's sparkling wine. These dolls are a decorative addition to a festive table. Bottle holders sometimes come apart in the middle like standard matryoshka dolls, sometimes

*Plate: 103 (opposite, above)*
*Title: Bread and Salt*
*City: Sergiev Posad*
*Artist: G. Sidorova*
*Size: 13-piece, 6 inches tall*
*The Russian symbol of hospitality on a grandmother doll adorned with a lace pattern.*

*Plate: 104 (opposite, below)*
*Size: 13-piece,7 inches tall*
*These grandmother dolls, which feature three generations (grandmother, mother, and granddaughter), are still relatively rare.*

*Plate: 105 (below)*
*Title: Bottle Holder Couple*
*Factory: Vyatski Souvenir, Nolinsk*
*Size: 1-piece, 12.5 inches tall and 13.5 inches tall*
*These dolls open near the bottom and are hollow so that a bottle of vodka fits inside.*

GZHELKA
КРИСТАЛЛ
БАЛЬЗАМ

open near the bottom, and sometimes open in two places, so that the drink can be poured while the bottle is still in the holder.

## Accessories and Toys

Matryoshka dolls have served as models for a variety of Russian gift items. For example, earrings shaped like matryoshki and painted as if they were tiny dolls are popular and inexpensive. Earrings are also painted as Santas, snowmen, or angels.

Another popular though unusual use of matryoshki as an item of wearable folk art is a lapel pin that resembles a large safety pin from which five little dolls hang. Usually, these five dolls line up from large to small, with the largest piece being about 0.75 inches high, and the smallest about 0.5 inches high. Like the earrings, these lapel pins come in various designs. Some are all Santas, some depict families (a father, mother, boy, girl, and usually a cat or dog), and some a series of Christmas items (for example a Santa, Snow Maiden, snowman, snow flake, and Christmas tree). Matryoshka dolls are also used in an increasingly wide variety of accessories, gifts and decorative items. Fobs for key chains and brightly-colored refrigerator magnets are just two examples.

There are also matryoshka-painting bears among the charming carved wooden toys called *bogorodskoye*. These delightful souvenirs, with an impressive folk craft tradition of their own, are named for the village where they originated and are still made. The bears are animated by a pull-string or by a string attached to a wooden ball that swings under the paddle-like base of the toy. The matryoshka artist bears move their arms to swing their brushes against the dolls in painting motions. The tongue-in-cheek cross fertilization between these two classic Russian folk crafts is another indication that Russian folk art is re-claiming its vibrancy.

*Plate: 106 (opposite)*
*Title: Bottle Holders*
*Vodka size: 12 inches tall*
*Champanskaya size: 14.5 inches*
*Collection: Gail Buyske*
*Widely used as gifts, these dolls are filled with a favorite bottle of vodka or wine.*

*Plate: 107 (above, top)*
*Title: Christmas Tree Ornaments*
*Size: 2.7 inches tall + clip*
*Collection: Gail Buyske*
*Molded glass ornaments in the shape of matryoshki can still be found in second-hand and commission stores in Russia.*

*Plate: 108 (above, left)*
*Title: Bogorodskoye Bears*
*Size: 5 inches tall*
*Collection: Jo Kessel Buyske*
*These popular toys do many things, but painting dolls is what got them into this book.*

*Plates: 109-117 (above), 118 (right)*
*City: Sergiev Posad*
*Earrings, lapel or sweater pins, refrigerator magnets, and keychains in the shape of matryoshki are all popular gifts.*

*Plate: 119 (opposite)*
*Title: Alice in Wonderland*
*Artist: M. Drozdova*
*Size: 10-piece, 9.5 inches tall*
*Collection: Odds & Ends Enterprises, Denver, Colorado*
*An English classic that lends itself well to the art of the matryoshka.*

## Matryoshka Themes

# A Story Within a Story

# Matryoshka Themes
## A Story Within a Story

It seems fitting that the "Gorby" doll heralded the explosion of matryoshka themes, since Gorbachev introduced the changes that have led to the freer economic and political system in Russia today. For nearly sixty years before Gorbachev, however, almost every matryoshka that was made featured flowers, with the occasional factory doll illustrating a folk theme. Today there is no limit to the themes, especially in dolls by independent artists. This chapter groups the ever evolving matryoshka themes into ten categories, beginning with flowers and concluding with today's newest themes.

### Flowers

Flowers appear on almost all matryoshki—on the fronts, on the scarves, on the aprons, or in the hair. Whether the theme is a fairy tale or folk tale, it is usually framed by flowers. The dolls that do not have flowers are those that portray famous people, such as political or religious subjects, or those that are Christmas oriented.

Although the most common flower painted on matryoshki is a stylized rose, many other flowers are also depicted, including daisies, lilies of the valley, and poppies. The simplest flowers are those painted in Maidan. They are outlined in black, and the red or pink paint often flows outside the black lines. The flowers are simply a series of flourishes that form a type of rose. The roses on other traditional dolls, from any of the factories, are more developed but still very simple. Natasha Grigorieva's flowers are made with just a few strokes of the brush, but they come out looking like little flowers. The most detailed flowers are those found on the most expensive dolls.

*Plate: 120 (chapter title)*
*Title: Alice in Wonderland*
*Artist: M. Drozdova*

*Plate: 121 (opposite)*
*Title: Palekh Scenes*
*Factory: Art Alliance, Kirov*
*Artist: R. Ivanova*
*Size: 10-piece, 9.7 inches tall*
*The medallion is a scene in the style of Palekh lacquer boxes.*

*Plate: 122 (above)*
*Title: Flowers*
*City: Moscow*
*Artist: V. Bogoslovsky*
*Size: 7-piece, 8 inches tall*
*The medallion on this doll is painted in the style of lacquer boxes and brooches from the city of Mstyora.*

Volodya Bogoslovsky's medallion with flowers is masterful; he borrows techniques from the classic lacquer boxes made in the village of Mstyora.

## Folk Tales

Although the Russian word *skazka* applies to both folk and fairy tales, the English language differentiation is still relevant. A folk tale is short and to the point, usually with a moral. It often takes place in a rural setting, its main characters are peasants and animals, and, in keeping with Russian tradition, it expresses a bit of peasant wisdom. A fairy tale is generally longer and almost always includes fantasy characters.

There are hundreds of traditional Russian folk tales, many of which have been portrayed on nesting dolls. The four most commonly pictured on matryoshki are *The Turnip (Repka), The Roll (Kolobok), The Tower (Teremok),* and *The Spotted Hen (Kurochka ryaba).* There are several matryoshka versions of each of these tales, a few of which are presented here.

Perhaps the most appropriate tale for a nesting doll is *The Turnip.* It is an engaging—and moralizing—tale about a Russian farmer who grew the biggest turnip in the world. When the farmer went to pull the turnip, it was so big that he could not get it out of the ground. So he called his wife, then his granddaughter, then the dog, then the cat. They all pulled, but still could not get the turnip out. Finally, they called a mouse, and when the mouse pulled, the turnip came out. The moral of the story is that no matter how small you are, you can still make a difference.

There are several nesting doll versions of *The Turnip.* The simplest are 5-piece dolls, although the logical number for the story is a 7-piece doll, with each of the six pieces representing a character from the story and the seventh representing the turnip. Some versions include a large turnip on the outside, while artist Sergei Koblov's version includes a small, carved turnip as the smallest piece. One of the most elaborate turnips is done by Vera Andreyeva. It is a hollowed-out turnip, complete with a wooden top in the shape of turnip greens. Inside are three characters—the grandpa, the grandma, and the granddaughter. Each of those characters has one other character inside—a little dog, cat, and mouse.

*Kolobok* is a word rarely used in modern Russian. It refers to a "roll." The folk tale *The Roll* is the Russian equivalent of *The Gingerbread Man.* In the Russian version (although like folk tales everywhere, there are myriad variations), an old lady makes a roll and then sets it on the windowsill to cool. The roll rolls away, singing a little song as he goes. He rolls past the rabbit and the bear, each of which wants to eat the roll. Finally, he rolls to the fox, who tells him that she likes his song, but she does not hear well. She asks him to jump up on her nose so that she can hear the song better, and there the roll meets his demise.

*Teremok* is also an archaic word. Literally, it is the diminutive of *terem,* "a tower of a castle."

*3 Plates combined (opposite)*

*Plate: 126 (top)*
*Title: The Turnip*
*City: St. Petersburg*
*Artist: TolsToys staff artist*
*Size: 7-piece, 7 inches tall*
*The outside doll is the large turnip, followed by the grandfather the grandmother, the granddaughter, the dog, the cat, and the mouse, whose help enables the group to pull the turnip out of the ground.*

*Plate: 127 (middle)*
*Title: Kolobok (The Roll)*
*Factory or City: Orekhovo-Zuyevo*
*Artist: S. Koblov workshop artist*
*Size: 5-piece, 6.5 inches tall*
*This version of the* Kolobok *was painted by one of Sergei Koblov's students.*

*Plate: 128 (bottom)*
*Title: Kolobok (The Roll)*
*Factory or City: St. Petersburg*
*Artist: N. Sokolova for TolsToys*
*Size: 5-piece, 6 inches tall*
*On this* Kolobok, *the fox devours the bun, then departs satisfied.*

*Plate: 129 (above)*
*Title: Kolobok (The Roll)*
*City: Sergiev Posad*
*Artist: V. Andreyeva*
*Size: 8-piece, 5.3 inches tall*
*Collection: Vicki Miller*
*The rabbit fits inside the bear, the fox inside the old lady, and the wolf inside the old man. They all fit inside the large kolobok, with the little bun that is eventually eaten by the fox.*

*Plate: 130 (left)*
*Title: Kolobok (The Roll)*
*Factory: Art Alliance, Kirov*
*Artist: Factory artists*
*Size: 7-piece, 6.3 inches tall*
*One of the simplest versions of this common folk tale, with a round roll as the innermost piece that looks just like the illustration on the outermost piece.*

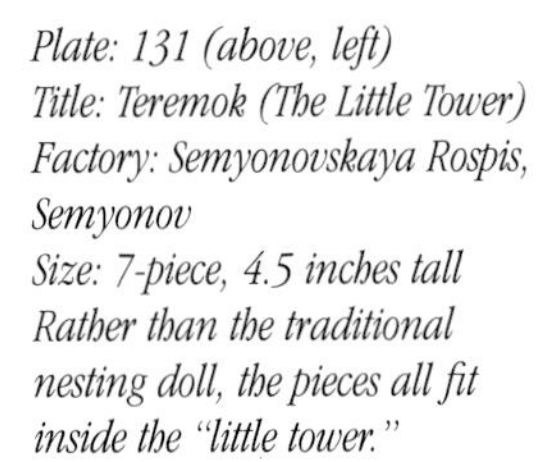

*Plate: 131 (above, left)*
*Title: Teremok (The Little Tower)*
*Factory: Semyonovskaya Rospis, Semyonov*
*Size: 7-piece, 4.5 inches tall*
*Rather than the traditional nesting doll, the pieces all fit inside the "little tower."*

*Plate: 132 (above, right)*
*Title: The Spotted Hen*
*Factory: Art Alliance, Kirov*
*Artist: Factory artists*
*Size: 4-piece, 4.5 inches tall*
*A simple doll for a simple story. The hen lays a golden egg, but when it falls on the floor, it turns into a plain egg and breaks. The hen tells her owners, an old couple, that from now on, she will provide them with an egg every day.*

Hence, although it is usually translated as *The Tower,* a better translation could be *The Cottage.* An insect is flying through the woods and sees a little cottage. He decides to move in. Then a mouse runs by, and the insect invites the mouse to come live with him in the cottage. The insect and mouse are joined by a rabbit and a frog and a wolf and a fox. Finally, a bear comes by, and the other cottage residents invite him to join them. The bear looks inside and sees that there is no room for him, so he goes up onto the roof, but the roof collapses. Fortunately, the animals are not hurt, and they all gather and decide to build a new, larger cottage to accommodate everyone. (The other version of the story is that the animals all run back into the forest, where they live happily every after.)

Finally, *The Spotted Hen* is the story of an elderly couple (not unlike the one in *The Roll*) who have a hen that has laid a golden egg. They sit and contemplate what to do with the egg, when a mouse runs across the table. When the egg falls on the floor, it breaks and turns out to be an ordinary egg. The hen tells the old couple not to worry because she will provide an egg for them every day—they will always have food to eat.

These are only a few of the folk tales that are illustrated on nesting dolls. There are countless others, including *Masha and the Bear, Animals at the Fence,* and *The Mitten* (a Ukrainian folk tale

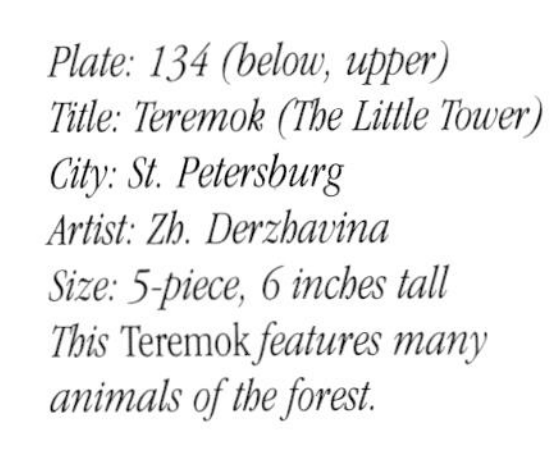

*Plate: 134 (below, upper)*
*Title: Teremok (The Little Tower)*
*City: St. Petersburg*
*Artist: Zh. Derzhavina*
*Size: 5-piece, 6 inches tall*
*This* Teremok *features many animals of the forest.*

*Plate: 135 (below, lower)*
*Title: Masha and the Bear*
*City: Orekhovo-Zuyevo*
*Artist: S. Koblov workshop artist*
*Size: 5-piece, 6.5 inches tall*
*Masha is taken prisoner by a bear in the woods. She tells him that her grandparents are hungry, and that she must bake them some meat pies for him to take to them. She hides in the basket with the pies, and the bear unwittingly takes her home.*

*Plate: 135 (near right)*
*Title: Ruslan and the Head*
*City: Moscow*
*Artist: M. Bogoslovskaya*
*Size: 10-piece, 9.5 inches tall*
*The miniature on the medallion of this doll is done in the style of Palekh lacquer boxes, and depicts the confrontation between Ruslan, who is looking for his beloved Lyudmila, and a huge head that has been condemned to life with no body. After Ruslan wins the battle, the head gives him information that will lead him to Lyudmila.*

*Plate: 136 (right)*
*Title: Fairy Tales*
*City: Moscow*
*Artist: M. Bogoslovskaya*
*Size: 7-piece, 8 inches tall*
*This has become a classic form for high end dolls – a beautiful face, an intricate scarf, and a medallion with intricate paintings of fairy tales.*

*Plate: 137 (between columns)*
*Title: Nutcracker micro*
*Size: 5-piece, 1.2 inches tall*
*Five nutcrackers packed into a tiny doll.*

*Plate: 138 (opposite)*
*Title: Fedoskino*
*Artist: Unknown*
*Size: 10-piece, 11 inches tall*
*Collection: Vicki Miller*
*The medallion on this elegant doll depicts scenes done in the style of Fedoskino lacquer boxes.* Potal *is used to frame the face and medallion.*

similar to *Teremok*). Some of the folk tales are not necessarily Russian in origin, although, like *The Roll,* folk tales often cross borders.

Curiously, there are also stories that are well known in Russia that do not appear on nesting dolls as frequently as one might expect. *Peter and the Wolf, The Nutcracker,* and *The Three Little Pigs* are examples of stories that seem to be natural subjects for nesting dolls, but they are rarely depicted.

## Fairy Tales

Not only are fairy tales longer and more fanciful than folk tales, but they are usually attributed to specific authors. Perhaps because of the complexity of fairy tales, they are most commonly depicted on nesting dolls as miniatures on medallions and therefore appear on expensive matryoshki. Often, these illustrations are copies of lacquer boxes, which frequently depict fairy tale themes, usually in the style of

Palekh artists. This style works well on matryoshki; it features fine painting on a black background. A black medallion stands out on any background color, and the miniature is well framed by the scarf.

There are three Russian authors who are well known for writing fairy tales. The best known is Russia's most revered author, Alexander Pushkin, who was a prolific writer of poetry and prose until he died in a duel at the age of 37 in 1837. Two authors who are known specifically for their fairy tales are Pyotr Ershov and Pavel Bazhov.

Pushkin recorded several fairy tales, but there are two that are most commonly depicted on nesting dolls, *Ruslan and Lyudmila* and *Tsar Saltan*. Each of these stories is quite long, consisting of several chapters. They are preceded by prologues, which are among the best loved passages of Russian literature. The prologue to *Ruslan and Lyudmila* is called "At the Bend in the Sea." It features a green oak to which a cat is chained ("when he goes to his left, he sings a song; when he goes to his right, he tells a tale"). This bend in the sea is the scene of many wondrous apparitions, including mermaids, invisible animals, and Baba Yaga in her house on two chicken legs. All of these themes have been painted on matryoshka dolls.

The prologue has little to do with the actual tale, however. *Ruslan and Lyudmila* begins with a wedding for the two title characters. During the celebration after the wedding, the bride is kidnapped by the evil Chernomor. Ruslan and three of his rivals go in search of the beautiful Lyudmila. Ruslan first must vanquish an enormous head that is blocking his way (another common theme on

*Plate: 139 (previous pages)*
*Size: 15-piece, 11 inches tall*
*Collection: Vicki Miller*
*This is an example of a matryoshka featuring scenes from a variety of Russian fairy tales, rather than following one particular story from beginning to end.*

*Plate: 140 (opposite)*
*Title: Fairy Tale Cutout*
*Size: 10-piece, 10 inches tall*
*Collection: Vicki Miller*
*The cutout shape occasionally is used for fairy tales rather than for religious themes. Note that because every other piece is used as a frame, the 10-piece doll appears to be only five pieces when fully displayed.*

*Plate: 141 (above)*
*City: Raduzhnoye*
*Artist: N. Pugaeva*
*Size: 5-piece, 6 inches tall*
*Collection: Vicki Miller*
*Illustrations of the story of* Tsar Saltan, *written by Alexander Pushkin.*

*Plate: 142*
*Title: The Humpbacked Pony*
*City: Sergiev Posad*
*Artist: Alekseyeva*
*Size: 7-piece, 8 inches tall*
*One of Russia's best loved fairy tales. The face on this doll is de-emphasized. The illustrations of the fairy tale continue on the back.*

matryoshka dolls) and then find Chernomor's castle, where Lyudmila is held captive. After riding through the air on Chernomor's beard, he rescues Lyudmila and returns home, where he immediately slays hundreds of invaders and saves his homeland.

The tale *Tsar Saltan* (the full name is *The Tale of Tsar Saltan, of his Son the Glorious and Powerful Knight Prince Gvidon Saltanovich, and of the Wonderful Swan Princess)* begins with the prologue "Three Maidens Under the Window." Here, three sisters are spinning wool when Tsar Saltan happens by their window (also often depicted on nesting dolls). One sister says that if she were married to the tsar, she would prepare him a wonderful feast. The second says that if she were married to him, she would weave him the finest cloth. The third says that she would bear him a brave son. The tsar marries the third sister and names the other two the royal seamstress and the royal cook. The other sisters are not happy with their fate. And so begins the story. The wife bears the tsar a son, but her sisters put her and her son (Gvidon) in a barrel and throw them in the sea. They are saved by a magic swan and end up living in a beautiful palace on an island that features, among other marvels, a squirrel that spends days cracking nuts made of gold to reveal the emerald kernels inside (also a common matryoshka theme). Slowly, Gvidon plans revenge on his aunts and returns to take over Tsar Saltan's empire.

Other Pushkin tales that are depicted on matryoshki include *The Tale of the Fisherman and the Fish*, *The Tale of the Golden Cockerel, The Tale of the Dead Princess and the Seven Knights* (Pushkin's version of the Grimm's tale *Snow White and the Seven Dwarves*), and, more rarely, *The Tale of the Preacher and His Worker Balda*.

*Plate: 143*
*Title: General Toptygin*
*Size: 5-piece, 6 inches tall*
*Collection: Vicki Miller*
*The story of the bear that drives a sleigh.*

One of the most beloved fairy tales in Russia is *The Humpbacked Pony* by Pyotr Ershov. It is a good story for nesting dolls, describing the adventures of a youngest son, Ivan. He has adopted a small, ugly pony who, it turns out, has magical powers. Ivan and the pony encounter a series of fantastic creatures. Among those creatures is a magic, fiery peacock-like bird, a "firebird." The strangest creature may be the he-she-fish whale (or more literally translated as a "miracle-foreign-fish-whale") that ran aground years ago and whose back is now the home of farms and villages. The character from this tale most commonly featured on matryoshki is the hunchbacked pony himself, who is only two feet high and has foot-long ears.

Finally, several complex tales attributed to Pavel Bazhov and which take place in Russia's Ural mountains (considered the dividing line between eastern and western Russia) are often pictured on nesting dolls. Among them are *The Mistress of Copper Mountain*, *The Malachite Box*, *The Stone Flower*, and *Silver Hoof*.

Tales that are familiar to non-Russians as well as Russians also find their way onto nesting dolls, including those written by the Brothers

*Plate: 144 (opposite)*
*Title: Alice in Wonderland*
*Artist: M. Drozdova*
*Size: 10-piece, 9.5 inches tall*
*Collection: Odds & Ends Enterprises, Denver, Colorado*
*An English classic that lends itself well to the art of the matryoshka.*

*Plate: 145 (above)*
*Title: Little Red Riding Hood*
*Size: 7-piece, 8 inches tall*
*Collection: Vicki Miller*
*This doll is an interesting example of a matryoshka doll without a face, apron, or medallion.*

*Plate: 146 (left)*
*Title: Cinderella*
*Size: 7-piece, 8 inches tall*
*Collection: Vicki Miller*
Cinderella, *a story as well known in Russia as it is elsewhere, is presented here in great detail.*

*Plate: 147 (above)*
*Title: 19th Century Borzoi Hunt*
*City: Rostov-on-Don*
*Artist: O. Sledkova*
*Size: 10-piece, 11 inches tall*
*Collection: The Russian Shop/ Maison Russe, Lisle, Illinois*
*A masterpiece with 61 borzois and 27 horses (4 dogs on the smallest doll alone). From a city not known for its nesting dolls.*

*Plate: 148 (right)*
*Title: Dogs*
*Factory: Vyatskii Souvenir, Nolinsk*
*Artist: Factory artists*
*Size: 5-piece, 5.5 inches tall*
*A simple dog doll.*

Grimm and Hans Christian Andersen. Some beautiful nesting dolls depict *Little Red Riding Hood*, *Cinderella*, and *The Snow Queen*.

## Animals

Animals appear frequently and in various ways on nesting dolls. Some of the most interesting depictions are somewhat stylized versions in which the face of the animal is where the face of the girl would be in a traditional doll. Such dolls include cats, dogs, and even such unlikely creatures as walruses, hippopotami, and frogs. Animals lend themselves well to micromats. The smallest piece in the micro penguin, which is only one quarter of an inch tall, wins everyone's heart.

Another commonly produced animal matryoshka is one that has a portrait on each piece. These are generally limited to cats, dogs, and horses. Most of these dolls have a matte finish. Generally, each piece of the nesting doll shows a different breed of the animal. The more artistic animal dolls have the name of the breed written on the back (in Russian).

Most of these animal dolls are produced southeast of Moscow in a city that is not generally known for its matryoshki, Ryazan. The city is in the

*Plate: 149 (above)*
*Title: Animals of the Forest*
*City: Sergiev Posad*
*Artist: Efremov*
*Size: 5-piece, 4 inches tall*
*Collection: Vicki Miller*
*Most animal dolls are simple portraits or caricatures; this little doll has a background to the animals.*

*Plate: 150 (left)*
*Title: Horse and Cat*
*City: Ryazan*
*Size: 5-piece, 6.5 inches tall*
*The artists of Ryazan paint realistic portraits of horses and cats on a light background. The back of the doll forms a dark brown frame.*

*Plate: 151 (top)*
*Title: Frog*
*City: St. Petersburg*
*Artist: Zh. Derzhavina*
*Size: 5-piece, 4 inches tall*
*Collection: Vicki Miller*
*The frog one of many animals to be depicted on nesting dolls, lends itself well to the pot-bellied shape.*

*Plae: 152 (middle)*
*Title: Micro Walrus*
*Factory or City: Sergiev Posad*
*Artist: Unknown*
*Size: 5-piece, 1.5 inches tall*
*Micromats lend themselves well to simple illustrations of animals.*

*Plate: 153 (bottom)*
*Title: Owl micro*
*Artist: Unknown*
*Size: 5-piece, 1.5 inches tall*
*Micromats feature not only owls, but also monkeys, walruses, and rhinoceroses.*

*Plate: 154 (above)*
*Title: Penguin micro*
*City: Sergiev Posad*
*Artist: L. and A. Kremnev*
*Size: 5-piece, 1.5 inches tall*
*The artist of this doll adds liveliness to the animal by using a purple color rather than the realistic black.*

*Plate: 155 (above)*
*Title: This Little Piggy*
*City: St. Petersburg*
*Artist: TolsToys staff artist*
*Size: 5-piece, 6 inches tall*
*Produced on request, this doll depicts an old American game usually played with a baby. "This little piggy went to market, this little piggy stayed home…"*

*Plate: 156 (left)*
*Title: Mother Cat*
*City: Dubna*
*Artist: Nikiforova*
*Size: 4-piece, 3 inches tall*
*This "mini-grandmother" is similar to the inside pieces of the grandmother doll, except that it has a base, indicating that it is the outside doll.*

*Plate: 157 (above)*
*Title: Peasant Family*
*Factory: Vyatskii Souvenir, Nolinsk*
*Artist: factory artist*
*Size: 9-piece, 7.2 inches tall*
*The objects are associated with Russian country life – the large stove, the teapot, the mushroom basket, the milk pot, and the water bucket.*

*Plate: 158 (right)*
*Title: Troika*
*City: Raduzhnoye*
*Artist: N. Pugaeva*
*Size: 5-piece, 6 inches tall*
Troikas *are frequently depicted in scenes of Russian country life.*

*Plate: 159 (opposite)*
*Title: Peasant Woman*
*City: Sergiev Posad*
*Artist: N. Kolesnikova*
*Size: 10-piece, 10.5 inches tall*
*Kolesnikova's charming peasant dolls start with either the husband or wife, and continue with other members of the family.*

general direction of Maidan, which may have influenced the beginning of Ryazan's matryoshka making. Besides the animal dolls, Ryazan artists specialize in portraits of famous people.

## Country Life

Many nesting dolls depict peasants. The name "matryoshka," after all, was a common peasant's name in the nineteenth century. One could argue that the standard matryoshka is a peasant, as few city dwellers wear the trademark scarf and apron of a nesting doll. The nesting dolls that we characterize as "peasant" might include animals such as cows, cats, or chickens, and may be carrying a pail of water or wood.

In addition to the peasants themselves, many matryoshki are painted with such subjects as *troikas,* winter scenes, or villages. These dolls

*Plate: 160 (opposite)*
*Title: The Art of Kustodiev*
*City: Moscow*
*Artist: Yu. Trembach*
*Size: 10-piece, 9 inches tall*
*Collection: Odds & Ends Enterprises, Denver, Colorado*
*Reproductions of the works of Boris Kustodiev—an early 20th-century Russian artist.*

*Plate: 161 (above)*
*Title: The Art of Vasnetsov*
*City: Sergiev Posad*
*Artist: Petrushin*
*Size: 10-piece, 10 inches tall*
*Collection: Vicki Miller*
*Reproductions of this 19th-century artist's most famous works, including* The Three Bogatyrs, Ivan Tsarevich and the Gray Wolf, *and* Alyonushka.

often feature quaint wooden houses or churches, and people in national dress. One common theme on nesting dolls—as well as other media—is a young couple, in which the girl is carrying a bucket of water and the boy is walking beside her.

## Reproductions of Fine Art

In addition to reproducing lacquer box artwork on matryoshki, many fine artists have reproduced classical paintings on matryoshka dolls. These dolls generally include several paintings done by the same artist. One such doll features reproductions of paintings done by one of Russia's favorite artists, Viktor Vasnetsov, best known for his paintings of knights on the battlefield and paintings from some fairy tales. Other art that has been copied onto nesting dolls includes: Marc Chagall's fanciful cities and landscapes, complete with colorful

(sometimes flying) cows; the work of Ivan Bilibin, the best known Russian illustrator of children's books; and the work of Kuzma Petrov-Vodkin, a Russian painter of the early twentieth century. Generally, these matryoshki reproduce works of Russian artists, rather than western European or other artists.

## Religion

Devout Russian Orthodox believers consider the depiction of an Orthodox icon on anything other than an icon to be sacrilegious. That said, many Russians and foreigners who are practicing Orthodox Christians purchase matryoshka dolls illustrated with copies of icons. There is no record of religious subjects on early matryoshki; perhaps this is because, before the 1917 revolution, Russian Orthodox Christians knew that copying such works was inappropriate.

Many religious dolls are exquisite. The artist V. I. Kuzmin, from Sergiev Posad, paints icon matryoshki that are luminescent. These dolls generally feature a Madonna and child on the outside piece, Jesus on the second piece, and then a series of saints on the last three pieces. The luminescence is achieved by using a layer of foil under the paint, just enough so that the paint acquires a metallic sheen. An egg-shaped matryoshka by an artist named Romanova, from the city of Ryazan, depicts the life of Christ.

Perhaps the most unusual of all religious matryoshki is the St. George, named for the depiction of St. George slaying the dragon, which is painted on the back of the doll. The outside piece of this doll is cut out so that the second piece can be seen beneath it. The icon, usually a Madonna and child, is therefore in a frame. In addition, there are smaller cutouts revealing angels on either side of the central one, creating a

*Plate: 161 (opposite)*
*Title: Madonna*
*Size: 10-piece, 10 inches tall*
*Collection: Vicki Miller*
*It appears that the woman on this doll is actually holding the icon.*

*Plate: 162 (above)*
*Title: Life of Christ*
*City: Raduzhnoye*
*Artist: N. Pugaeva*
*Size: 5-piece, 6 inches tall*
*Collection: Vicki Miller*
*A series of scenes from the New Testament.*

triptych. In a 10-piece doll, every other piece is cut out, so that the 2nd, 4th, 6th, 8th, and 10th pieces appear to be inside frames of the 1st, 3rd, 5th, 7th, and 9th. Although it is a 10-piece doll, it would appear, when displayed with every other doll nested to show the framing, as only 5 pieces.

*Plate: 163 (opposite, above)*
*Title: Madonna and Child*
*City: Ryazan*
*Artist: E. Struevich*
*Size: 7-piece, 7 inches tall*
*Collection: Vicki Miller*
*These cutout nesting dolls, which give the impression of an icon in a frame, require a skilled woodworker as well as a skilled matryoshka painter.*

*Plate: 164 (opposite, below)*
*Title: Christ and Saints*
*Size: 5-piece, 6 inches tall*
*Collection: Vicki Miller*
*Christ and a series of saints, carved and lacquered.*

*Plate: 165 (above)*
*Title: Madonnas*
*City: Sergiev Posad*
*Size: 20-piece, 12 inches tall*
*Collection: Donna and David Cattell-Gordon*
*This large doll features many different Madonnas. On the back of the larger pieces are verses written in Old Church Slavonic.*

*Plate: 166 (above)*
*Title: Jerusalem Characters*
*Artist: O. Drevina*
*Size: 10-piece, 10 inches tall*
*A beautiful doll featuring Jewish subjects.*

*Plate: 167 (left)*
*Title: The Tailor and the Rabbi*
*City: Sergiev Posad*
*Size: 1-piece* nevalyashka*,*
*4.5 inches tall*
*These are among a series of bells portraying Jewish characters.*

*Plate: 168 (above)*
*Title: Madonna and Child*
*City: Sergiev Posad*
*Artist: V. Kuzmin*
*Size: 5-piece, 6 inches tall*
*Kuzmin's saints are based on icons, with various background colors.*

*Plate: 169 (left)*
*Title: Nativity*
*City: Dubna*
*Artist: I. Gracheva*
*Size: 14-piece, 6 inches tall*
*Inside this sphere from Dubna are several traditional characters in a nativity scene – Jesus, Joseph, Mary, wise men and angels.*

*Plate: 170(below)*
*Title: Life of Christ*
*City: Raduzhnoye*
*Artist: N. Pugaeva*
*Size: 7-piece, 7.5 inches tall*
*Collection: Vicki Miller*
*One of Natasha Pugaeva's renditions of the life of Christ.*

*Plate: 171 (opposite)*
*Title: St. George*
*Size: 10-piece, 12 inches tall*
*Collection: Vicki Miller*
*The name of this doll derives from the painting on the back, showing St. George slaying the dragon.*

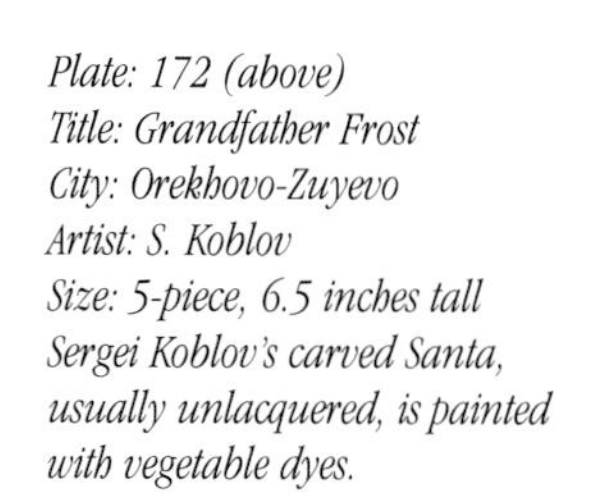

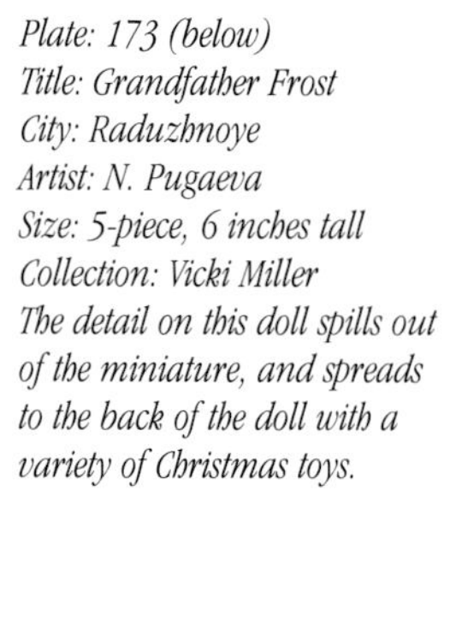

*Plate: 172 (above)*
*Title: Grandfather Frost*
*City: Orekhovo-Zuyevo*
*Artist: S. Koblov*
*Size: 5-piece, 6.5 inches tall*
*Sergei Koblov's carved Santa, usually unlacquered, is painted with vegetable dyes.*

*Plate: 173 (below)*
*Title: Grandfather Frost*
*City: Raduzhnoye*
*Artist: N. Pugaeva*
*Size: 5-piece, 6 inches tall*
*Collection: Vicki Miller*
*The detail on this doll spills out of the miniature, and spreads to the back of the doll with a variety of Christmas toys.*

## Christmas and Father Frost

Santa dolls are a new and widespread development in matryoshka production. In Russian, Santa is called *Ded moroz*, "Grandfather Frost." Grandfather Frost's helper is *Snegurochka*, the Snow Maiden. Therefore, many of the Santa dolls have Snow Maidens inside. There are two Snow Maidens in Russian lore, which can create some confusion. One is Santa's helper; the other is the subject of a fairy tale. In the fairy tale, a childless couple adopts the Snow Maiden, a statue of snow they find in the woods in winter. She becomes a real person and falls in love with a young man of the village named Lel. In the spring, she goes outside to see her beloved and melts away.

The production of Santa matryoshki has expanded rapidly, largely because of their popularity in the United States. They range in size from tiny micromats to at least 15-piece dolls that are about a foot high. Some are exceedingly simple, some quite complex.

*Plate: 174 (above)*
*Title: Grandfather Frost*
*Size: 5-piece, 6.5 inches tall*
*This brightly colored carved Santa is a children's favorite.*

*Plate: 175*
*Title: Korobeinik*
*City: Moscow*
*Size: 6-piece, 6 inches tall*
*The* korobeinik *looks like a nesting doll on the outside, but it has Christmas ornaments on the inside.*

*Plate: 176 (above)*
*Title: Santa*
*Size: 15-piece, 11 inches tall*
*An unusually large Santa.*

*Plate: 177 (right)*
*Title: Santa 10-piece micro*
*Size: 10-piece, 2 inches tall*
*This little Santa features feet on the bottom of the largest piece, and a little Christmas tree in the middle (or at least a piece painted green with a white garland).*

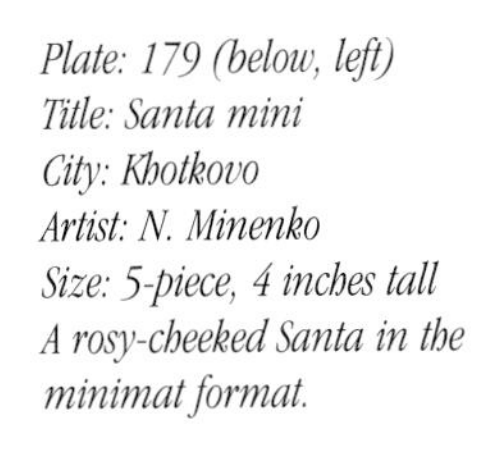

*Plate: 178 (above)*
*Title: Christmas Scenes*
*City: Sergiev Posad*
*Artist: Ye. Chudnova*
*Size: 5-piece, 5 inches tall*
*Yelena Chudnova's pastel blue background frames a series of winter scenes, starting with a charming Santa.*

*Plate: 179 (below, left)*
*Title: Santa mini*
*City: Khotkovo*
*Artist: N. Minenko*
*Size: 5-piece, 4 inches tall*
*A rosy-cheeked Santa in the minimat format.*

*Plate: 180 (below)*
*Title: Santa Scene*
*City: Sergiev Posad*
*Artist: Valery Aleksandrovsky*
*Size: 1-piece, 1 inch tall*
*This variation on the micromat is just one piece, with a little scene inside.*

## POLITICS

Political themes have a long tradition, beginning with renditions of Napoleon and Kutuzov that were created in 1912 by I. G. Prokhorov to commemorate the one hundredth-year anniversary of Russia's defeat of Napoleon. (Kutuzov was a Russian field marshal who was a key figure in the Russian victory.)

Plate: 181 (above)
Plate: 182 (opposite)
Title: Tsars of Russia
City: Ryazan
Artist: A. Strusswig
Size: 10-piece, 9 inches tall
Collection: Rett and Tania Ertl
This doll consists of portraits of the famous Romanov rulers, with names and dates of each inscribed on the back.

Political matryoshki have continued to evolve with the changing leadership. Not long after Boris Yeltsin succeeded Mikhail Gorbachev, the Yeltsin doll appeared. There was even a brief period when one could find Gorbachev dolls with Yeltsin on the inside, signifying Yeltsin's positon before he ousted Gorbachev and became the outside doll. (Under Gorbachev, Yeltsin was briefly removed from the inner circle.) And even before Vladimir Putin became president, the Putin doll appeared. These dolls most commonly have seven pieces—Putin, Yeltsin, Gorbachev, Brezhnev, Khrushchev, Stalin, and Lenin. Five-piece Putin dolls are also common, even though they leave out two important leaders of the Soviet Union. Ten-piece "Soviet leaders" matryoshki are also relatively common. They do not generally depict lesser known leaders like Konstantin Chernenko or Yuri Andropov, but rather include Nicholas II, Catherine the Great, and Peter the Great. Some have three small pieces that presumably represent tsars but are really unidentifiable. On the other hand, there are some beautiful matryoshki picturing the tsars of the Romanov dynasty.

The most popular Soviet leader dolls are done in caricature, showing Putin with his penetrating blue eyes, Yeltsin with his bulbous nose, Gorbachev with his birthmark, Khrushchev with an ear of corn, Stalin with his pipe, and Lenin with a red star. (After a trip to Iowa, Khrushchev tried to introduce corn into the Moscow region, forgetting that Iowa's climate is much warmer than Moscow's. This and similar projects contributed to Khrushchev's removal as the leader of the Soviet Union.)

The artists of Ryazan have come up with a process that allows them to produce very realistic portraits. The artists deny that the portraits are decals, but each painting is so similar that it is hard to believe that they are done freehand.

The success of the Soviet leader matryoshki has led to other ideas. First, dolls appeared picturing recent American presidents. Another doll shows Russian presidents on one side and American presidents on the other. In 1999, Bill Clinton dolls became the most popular political matryoshki. These show Clinton on the outside, with a cast of related characters on the inside, including Monica Lewinsky, Paula Jones, Gennifer Flowers, and usually Hillary Clinton. Other versions include a saxophone or a cigar.

*Plate: 183 (above)*
*Title: Russian Leaders*
*Size: 7-piece, 8 inches tall*
*Russian Leaders continues the tradition of the Gorby doll. All of the major Soviet leaders (Lenin, Stalin, Khrushchev, Brezhnev, and Gorbachev) and the two post-Soviet presidents (Yeltsin and Putin) are included.*

*Plate: 184 (right)*
*Title: Gorbachev Era*
*Size: 7-piece, 8 inches tall*
*Collection: Gail Buyske*
*This is an unusual doll, created before Yeltsin became president, with Yeltsin shown as smaller than Gorbachev.*

*Plate: 185 (above)*
*Title: Clinton and his Girls*
*City: Ryazan*
*Size: 5-piece, 6 inches tall*
*Although Ryazan artists deny it, it appears that they use a transfer process to get realistic portraits on these matryoshki.*

## Turning to New Markets

As Russia began the transition to a market economy in the early 1990s, matryoshka exports to foreign countries grew. And as tourism increased, at least to Russia's major cities of Moscow and St. Petersburg, makers and sellers of matryoshki quickly responded to the tastes and interests of foreign buyers.

Matryoshki entered foreign, and specifically American, culture in two ways. First, they began depicting American subjects. Second, they started appearing in American film and television.

Besides the previously mentioned American presidents, many other American subjects grace matryoshki. Probably the most popular subjects are cartoon characters, especially from Disney and Warner Brothers. Among cartoon character dolls, the most popular is the Winnie the Pooh, which generally includes Eeyore, Rabbit, Owl, and Piglet. But on any given day at Izmailovsky Park, the outdoor craft market and favorite shopping area of foreign tourists, one can find a variety of American cartoon characters: Tom and Jerry, Snow White and the Seven Dwarves (which, by the way, works very well on a matryoshka doll), Mickey Mouse, and the Flintstones.

Almost as popular as cartoon characters are NFL, NBA, and NHL teams. The most popular team from the United States is probably the Chicago Bulls starring Michael Jordan, even after their period of domination of the NBA. It is difficult to say why so many artists produce the Bulls. Perhaps it is because their string of championships occurred as the Soviet Union was opening up and therefore coincided with the creation of the first NBA matryoshki. The second most popular matryoshka sports team in Russia is the Detroit Red Wings,

HONEY

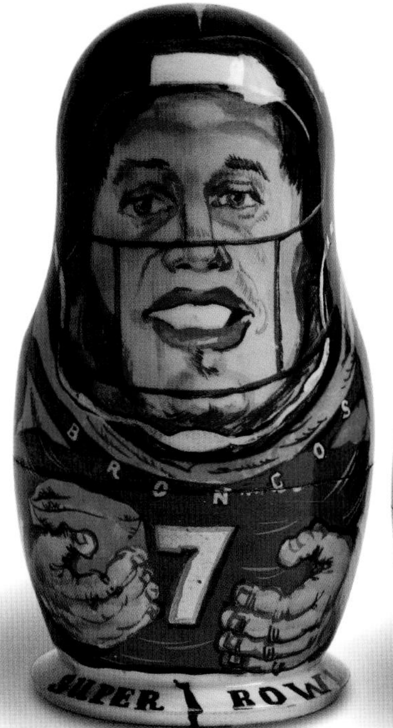

*Plate: 186 (opposite, top)*
*Title: Yellow Submarine*
*City: St. Petersburg*
*Artist: Golden Cockerel Crafts staff artists*
*Size: 5-piece, 5.5 inches tall, 6.5 inches long*
*A clever use of the matryoshka shape to create a submarine, which holds portraits of each of the Beatles.*

*Plate: 187 (opposite, bottom)*
*Title: Pooh micro*
*Size: 5-piece, 1.5 inches tall*
*An unlicensed but popular micro, this Pooh includes likenesses of Tigger, Eeyore, Owl, and Piglet. The last two are barely recognizable, but it is the idea that pleases people.*

as it is the hockey team featuring the most Russian players. However, since these matryoshki are primarily sold to foreign tourists, the supply is presumably related to demand. In any case, because most sports team dolls are sold to foreigners, the sellers of sports matryoshki offer a large selection of teams. That way, any sports fan can find his or her team.

Almost every aspect of American pop culture is represented on matryoshki. Celebrities from Elvis to Madonna, Marilyn Monroe to Britney Spears, and Kiss to U2 have been depicted on matryoshka dolls. Characters from *Star Trek* have been done, as have characters from *Star Wars*.

Artists have also painted their dolls in various professions and nationalities to appeal to tourists' or collectors' interests. The cobbler and tailor shown in this chapter are two examples. TolsToys produces matryoshki of doctors, teachers, judges, chefs, and nannies. The characterizations are as widely varying as the artists' styles, ranging from silly to serious likenesses. And, for customers wishing to commission a specific idea, dolls are painted with portraits of individuals, families, groups, or any subject imaginable.

*Plate: 188 (above)*
*Title: Denver Broncos Super Bowl Team*
*Size: 7-piece, 7.5 inches tall*
*An unlicensed doll that portrays the Broncos' Super Bowl team of 1999.*

*Plate: 189 (left)*
*Title: Colorado Avalanche*
*Size: 5-piece, 6 inches tall*
*Collection: Vicki Miller*
*One of many unlicensed dolls depicting American professional sports teams.*

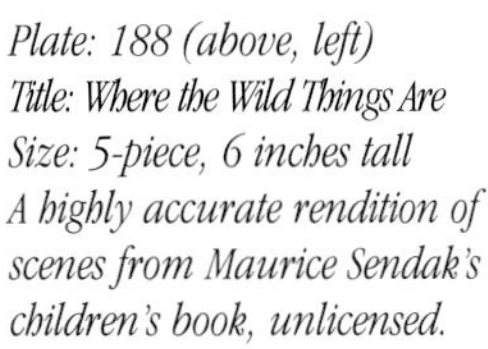

*Plate: 188 (above, left)*
*Title: Where the Wild Things Are*
*Size: 5-piece, 6 inches tall*
*A highly accurate rendition of scenes from Maurice Sendak's children's book, unlicensed.*

*Plate: 189 (above, right)*
*Title: Jurassic Park*
*City: Ryazan*
*Artist: Milashova*
*Size: 10-piece, 10 inches tall*
*Collection: Odds & Ends Enterprises, Denver, Colorado*
*One of America's blockbuster movies is transformed into an artful nesting doll.*

Photographs are sent to the artists for likeness. For example, commissions have been done of wedding parties as favors for the guests.

Copyright issues have historically not been a concern of Russian matryoshka artists and manufacturers. Property of any type, including intellectual property, was considered a capitalist concept during the Soviet period and has not yet become a major focus of Russian law-makers, not to mention craftspeople. As a result, none of the dolls mentioned above has been licensed.

TolsToys has taken the initiative to address this situation and to obtain such licenses. For example, the company has the license to produce dolls reproducing illustrations from Chris Van Allsburg's *The Polar Express*, one of the most popular children's Christmas books ever written. The company also produces matryoshki matching the doll in the American children's book *The Magic Nesting Doll*, written by Jacqueline Ogburn and

illustrated by Laurel Long.

In other cases, Americans are using matryoshki to market their own products. Golden Cockerel Crafts, in North Carolina and St. Petersburg, produced 40,000 matryoshki with characters from the movie *Being John Malkovich*. The movie itself involved characters inside of John Malkovich's head, so a matryoshka doll was natural for promoting the movie. Golden Cockerel was able to produce such a large number of matryoshki because they developed a machine to print a design on the doll. They also produced a smaller number of dolls to promote *The Drew Carey Show*.

Another example of the commercial application of the art of the matryoshka is in the advertising of the Ford Motor Company, which used animated nesting dolls to show the versatility of the 2001 Focus model.

In 2001, Madam Alexander, one of America's foremost manufacturers of collectible porcelain

*Plate: 190 (above, left)*
*Title: The Cobbler*
*City: Raduzhnoye*
*Artist: N. Pugaeva*
*Size: 5-piece, 6 inches tall*
*Collection: Vicki Miller*
*A Russian cobbler plies his trade.*

*Plate: 191 (above, right)*
*Title: Male Judge*
*City: St. Petersburg*
*Artist: TolsToys staff artist*
*Size: 5-piece, 6 inches tall*
*The innermost piece is a prisoner.*

*Plate: 192 (opposite)*
*Title: Madam Alexander*
*Size: 3-piece, 8 inches tall*
*Collection: Vicki Miller*
*In 2000, the venerable maker of porcelain dolls packaged a porcelain doll in Russian costume, and a small wooden doll, inside a matryoshka shell.*

*Plate: 193 (above)*
*Title: Bride and Groom*
*City: St. Petersburg*
*Artist: I. Gumnitsky*
*Size: 5-piece, 6 inches tall*
*A wedding gift with a touch of irony—the middle piece is a baby.*

*Plate: 194 (left)*
*Title: Hawaiian Girl*
*City: St. Petersburg*
*Artist: Nickolai Gurgeiff staff artist*
*Size: 5-piece, 6 inches tall*
*Produced by a company called Nickolai Gurgeiff, the Hawaiian Girl is popular among visitors to the islands.*

dolls, designed a nesting doll to go with one of their porcelain dolls. The outermost doll contains both the porcelain figure and a small 1-piece matryoshka, dressed in the same pattern and colors.

Russian nesting dolls have appeared in their own right in the American media. The movie *The Man Who Knew Too Little,* starring Bill Murray, features a bomb hidden in a nesting doll. A toy in the animated film *Toy Story* is a nesting dog. Millions of American children learned to count with the help of Sesame Street's nesting dolls. The next generation of matryoshka lovers is already growing up.

П. Чайковский
Мусоргский
Глинка

А.С. Пушкин
Толстой
Достоевский
Чехов

*Plate: 195 (previous left page)*
*Title: Russian Composers*
*City: Ryazan*
*Size: 5-piece, 6 inches tall*
*Realistic portraits of some of Russia's best known composers:*
*Tchaikovsky (top, left),*
*Mussorgsky (top, right)*
*Rachmaninoff (bottom, left)*
*Glinka (bottom, middle)*
*Prokofiev (bottom, right)*

*Plate: 196 (previous right page)*
*Title: Russian Authors*
*City: Ryazan*
*Size: 5-piece, 6 inches tall*
*Portraits of some of Russias favorite authors:*
*Pushkin (top, left)*
*Tolstoy (top, right)*
*Turgenev (bottom, left)*
*Dostoyevsky (bottom, middle)*
*Chekhov (bottom, right)*

*Plate: 197 (right)*
*(background)*
*Title: Inscribed Minimat*
*City: Sergiev Posad*
*Artist: M. Krivoshein*
*Size: 5-piece, 3 inches tall*
*Themes or other sentiments are not only expressed in the artwork, but sometimes in unexpected details. Maybe the artist was sending a message: "What do you want to be, brother? I want to be a writer, do you understand, brother?"*
*(foreground)*
*Title: Inscribed Minimat*
*City: Sergiev Posad*
*Artist: M. Krivoshein*
*Size: 5-piece, 3 inches tall*
*The artwork on this minimat is not unusual, but the inscription on the bottom is: "I'm gonna love you, too the heavens stop the rain." The English is not very good, either.*

# The Cities and Factories
# Made in the Russian Motherland

„Ах ты зимушка

# The Cities and Factories
## Made in the Russian Motherland

Russia today has five centers of matryoshka production, ranging from Sergiev Posad, an hour outside of Moscow, to Nolinsk, a very long day's drive away in the Kirov oblast. Several other factories, including one in the city of Yoshkar-Ola, capital of the Autonomous Republic of Mari-El, were closed in the mid-1990s.

This chapter begins where matryoshki began, with the small factories of Sergiev Posad, followed by Maidan, now known primarily for its backyard production of blanks. The three other cities, Semyonov, Kirov and Nolinsk, all produce matryoshki on a larger scale, including making their own blanks, but with marked variations in design and approach. While at first it seems sad that the Sergiev Posad factories have not been able to maintain the large-scale output of their competitors, the silver lining is the number of independent artists who now work in and around Sergiev Posad and who continue to experiment with expanding the matryoshka tradition.

*Plate: 198 (chapter title)*
*Title: Maidan Main Street*
*City: Polkhovsky Maidan*

*Plate: 199 (opposite)*
*Title: Oh, Winter!*
*Artist: I. Romanova*
*Size: 7-piece, 6 inches tall*

*Plate: 200 (above)*
*City: Sergiev Posad*
*The monastery has been a site of pilgrimage and tourism for centuries. This main gate faces the village across a vast square. On most days, the square is filled with artists and vendors selling dolls and other handcrafts.*

## Sergiev Posad

Sergiev Posad has four small "factories," each with under twenty artists and only two of which still produce some of their own blanks. The oldest factory is aptly named Factory No. 1, followed in order of founding dates by Souvenir, AOFIS (the Joint Stock Factory of Toys and Souvenirs) and Sergievskaya Igrushka (Sergiev Toys). All of these factories produce the Sergiev Posad dolls that resemble those that were produced during the years of Soviet rule. However, perhaps in a nod to modern life, each of the factories has at least one "author" artist, who paints in a distinct style. This chapter describes the factories;

## Western Russia and The Matryoshka Trail

The cities and villages of the matryoshka are within two days' drive of Moscow, but mostly over two-lane rural roads that make the journey long and even perilous, particularly in winter. The highlighted route is that taken by the authors

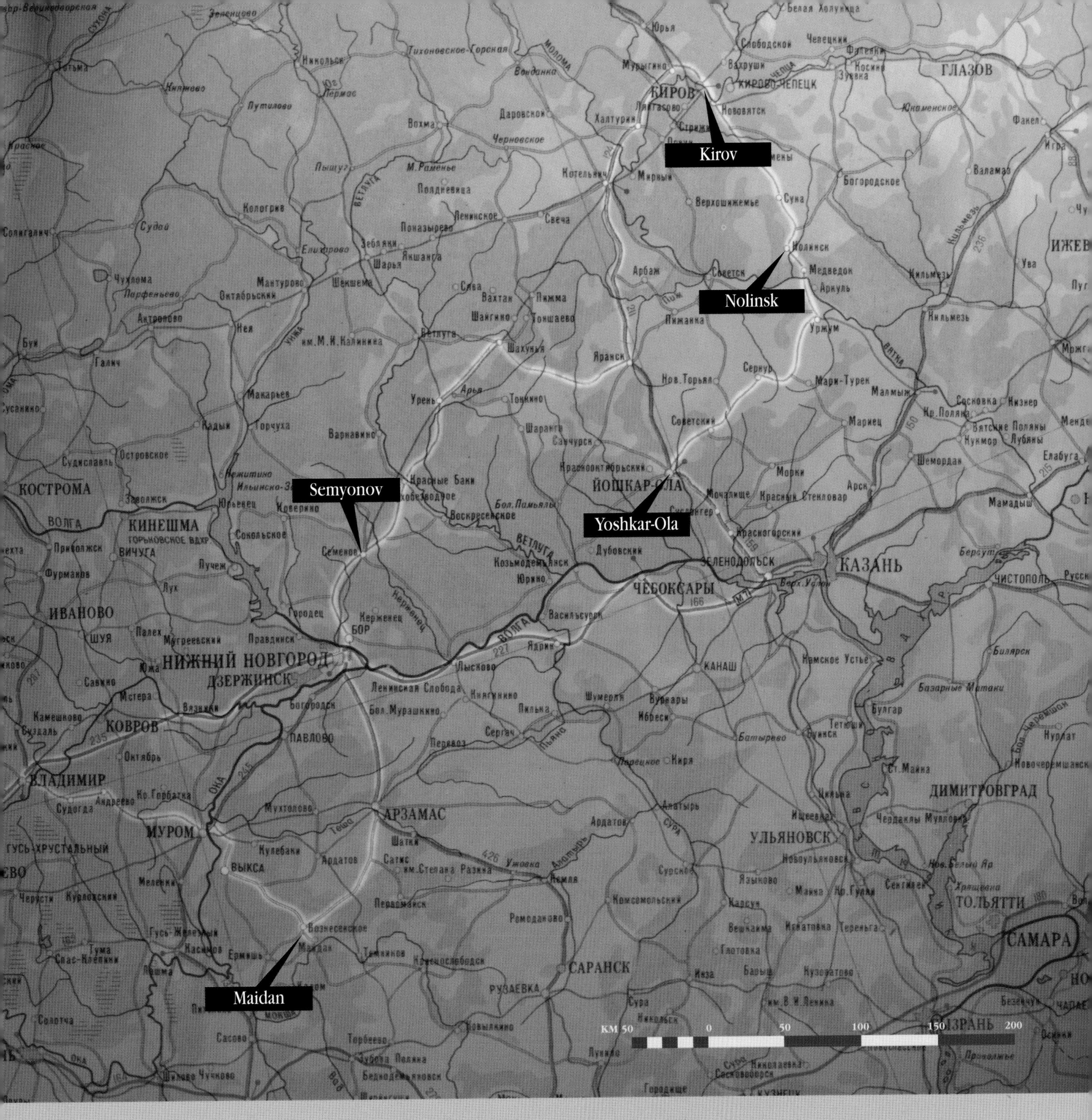


in the fall of 2001. The pictures in this book represent the factories and cities as they were at that time. Yet, judging from appearances, much has remained unchanged for many years—and will remain so for many more.

*Plate: 201 (above)*
*Title: Roadmap of western Russia and The Matryoshka Trail*

*Plate: 202 (inset)*
*Title: Map of Russia, with area of detail*

*Plates: 203, 204, 205, 206*
*Title: Woman painting scarves*
*Factory: Factory No. 1, Sergiev Posad*
*(top, left) Experienced artists share the workshop in Factory No. 1 with younger women who are still learning their craft.*
*(bottom, left) This woman paints the scarf freehand, creating a round face in the middle.*
*(top, right) Size: 1-piece, 12 inches tall;* Bogatyrs, *two knights errant, one with his shield.*
*(bottom, right) The first coat of paint to the matryoshka. This yellow layer will become the blouse, although only a small area in the front will show.*

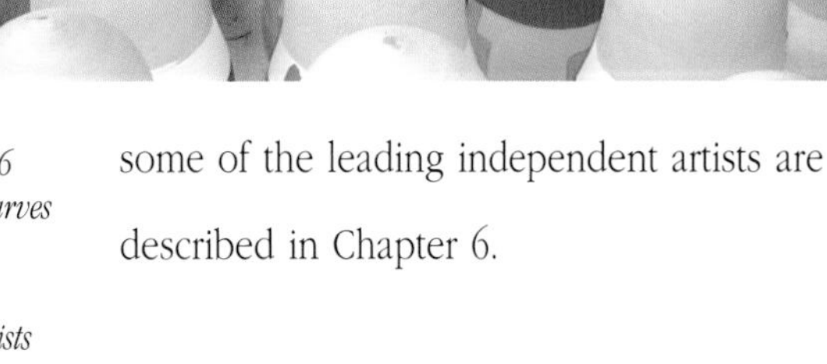

some of the leading independent artists are described in Chapter 6.

## Factory No. 1

Factory No. 1 is now officially The Closed Joint Stock Company of Artistic Products and Toys. Nevertheless, everyone still calls it Factory No. 1. The factory traces its origins to the first *zemstvo* workshop that was organized in Sergiev Posad in 1904. It is also the direct descendant of the RKKA factory, which was formed in 1930 from all of the private workshops in Sergiev Posad. During the Soviet period, Factory No. 1 was actually housed in the Trinity-Sergiev Monastery. It moved across the street in 1988.

Factory No. 1 still retains ties to the past; its director, Georgy Davydoch Argun, assumed his position in 1977. His secretary's mother was the lacquerer in the factory for 45 years, recently retiring from that position to become a receptionist.

Today, Factory No. 1 has only a few artists, in contrast to its proud 100-year history.

## Souvenir

When I first visited Souvenir in 1995, the factory still undertook all aspects of matryoshka production and occupied three floors. On the first floor, workers split logs using axes. There were six lathes to turn the blanks. The administration occupied the second floor and the artists painted traditional dolls, yet with a distinctive Souvenir style, on the third floor.

*Plate: 207 (far left)*
*Title: Workshop*
*Factory: Souvenir Factory, Sergiev Posad*
*Like the other Sergiev Posad factories, Souvenir employs only a few artists to produce its traditional dolls.*

*Plate: 208 (near left)*
*Title: Santas to be lacquered*
*Factory: Souvenir Factory, Sergiev Posad*
*Size: 5-piece, 5 inches tall*
*These Santas have been painted, and are waiting for the lacquerer to protect the surface and make them glossy.*

Souvenir has now shrunk to a considerably smaller operation. An art gallery largely occupies the first floor. There are a few matryoshka dolls, wooden toys, and other handcrafted items for sale, but most of the store is filled with oil and watercolor paintings. The second floor is leased out to a law office and to the regional headquarters of a Russian political party–itself an interesting change from the Russia of only a few years earlier. Souvenir is relegated to the third floor. One end of the floor houses the director's office (also doubling as the warehouse), as well as the bookkeeper's office, which is a small cubbyhole. On the other end are the painting room and the lacquer room. I have been to Souvenir when no artists

*Plate: 209 (below)*
*Title: Matryoshki*
*Factory: Souvenir Factory, Sergiev Posad*
*Size: 5-piece, 5 inches tall*
*The Souvenir factory produces traditional Sergiev Posad dolls.*

*Plate: 210*
*Factory: AOFIS, Sergiev Posad*
*The entrance to the office at AOFIS is framed by a birch tree, one of the national symbols of Russia, and a linden, the primary wood for matryoshki.*

were working there. Happily, on my latest visit there were a number of artists producing some appealing matryoshki.

## AOFIS

AOFIS is one of the smallest factories operating in Russia in terms of sales volume, having significantly shrunk since the glory days of the 1980s. Although AOFIS would like more business, whether it could produce more dolls if demand went up is uncertain at best. Most of the company's revenue now comes from the sale of plastic toys and other molded household items like buckets and pans.

AOFIS is among the most Soviet in style of all the matryoshka factories in Russia. There is no marketing department as such, and managers talk about orders as if they fall from the sky. In fact, AOFIS sells most of its dolls to *perekupchiki* – literally, rebuyers. These are not considered real customers but the bane of socialist existence – middlemen. These *perekupchiki* buy the matryoshki made at AOFIS and sell them, mostly in Moscow, especially at Izmailovsky Park. Such an arrangement is not yet universally accepted in Russia.

Ironically, despite AOFIS's low sales volume, it is one of only two factories in Sergiev Posad that still makes some of its own blanks. But, whereas AOFIS used to receive linden logs that had been felled in the vicinity of Sergeiv Posad, and which were supplied by the state, now most of the lindens in the region have been harvested. AOFIS carries on nonetheless, air drying some logs in an open shed and employing one man to take the logs from the shed, saw them to the proper length and operate the preliminary lathe. There are three finishing lathes and three operators, including a woman who began her career at Factory No. 1.

While AOFIS artists use primary colors in their work, the only rule that I could determine is that the matryoshka sleeves are always yellow. The paint is gouache, a thickened watercolor that is opaque, so that the grain of the wood does not show through.

## Sergievskaya Igrushka

The founder of Sergievskaya Igrushka, Valentina Vladimirovna Bakulina, was a former director of the Souvenir Factory. After the fall of the Soviet Union, Valentina decided to form her own production company, rather than wait for Souvenir to adapt to the new market economy. She did so with some of the artists from Souvenir as well as from Factory No. 1.

In 1995 Valentina turned the operations over to two younger employees, Maria Borisovna Dain (Masha) and Svetlana Vladmirovna Pankova (Sveta), who now manage the company and actively sell its products, including outside of Russia. They also market folk art products made in and around Sergiev Posad, but matryoshki are still their primary product. Sergievskaya Igrushka owns a lathe, but produces only a limited number of blanks.

Superficially, Sergievskaya Igrushka appears no different than its competitors. It is housed in the administrative offices of a former stadium, it employs only ten artists, and produces traditional Sergiev Posad matryoshki. However, Sergievskaya Igrushka has no unused space, there is a strong sense of focus, and it is clear that this is a business with an eye on the future.

## Maidan

The village of Polkhovsky Maidan, located about eight hours by car southeast of Moscow, is the center of Russia's matryoshka blank production. One could easily wonder why: Maidan is far from a major city and is not located in a dense linden

*Plate: 211 (far left)*
*Factory: AOFIS, Sergiev Posad*
*Many of these women have been painting matryoshki for all of their adult lives. Their experience translates into flawless matryoshki.*

*Plate: 212 (above)*
*Factory: AOFIS, Sergiev Posad*
*One by one, the artist adds new details on each doll.*

*Plate: 213 (above)*
*City: Maidan*
*The linden groves surrounding the village of Maidan have been harvested, but the forest is still relatively close. The yards, like most rural Russian houses, include a vegetable garden.*

*Plate: 214 (inset)*
*City: Maidan*
*Behind nearly all the houses in Maidan are sheds with lathes in them. Linden logs can be seen throughout the village, stacked vertically for drying until they are ready to be turned into blanks.*

forest. The best, albeit partial, answer comes from Pyotr Fyodorov, one of the senior lathe operators of the village, who has been making matryoshki since he was ten. As he put it, "My father was a woodworker, as was my grandfather, as was my great-grandfather."

Every matryoshka specialist makes a point of saying that the commercial nature of the Nizhny Novgorod region, in which Maidan is located, contributed to the development of the craft industry in that area. Perhaps a Maidan craftsman was at the Nizhny Novgorod market a hundred years ago and brought home the idea of a nesting doll. For whatever reason, Maidan has been a woodworking village for at least one hundred years and probably much longer. At some point, this skill was adapted to the production of matryoshka dolls. During the Soviet period, Maidan and Semyonov were the two largest producers of matryoshki. However, the Maidan factory was closed some time ago.

There may be a dozen streets in Maidan and nearly every house has a shed behind it or in

*Plate: 215 (above)*
*City: Maidan*
*This is Pyotr Fyodorov's lathe room. Like most in Maidan, he has built his own machinery, maintains it, and keeps his tools sharp. Sweeping the floor, however, is not a major concern.*

*Plate: 216 (left)*
*City: Maidan*
*In Maidan, the bottom piece of a doll is customarily made first. Here, Pyotr removes the wood from the inside of a top piece. The steel tool rest parallel to the workpiece is set into a solid block of hardwood, held to the bench with wooden wedges.*

front with a homemade lathe inside – basically a motor with a spinning axle. Every male resident in Maidan operates a lathe. It is simply something that you do if you live there and it offers a good living. If you are a boy in Maidan and would like to do anything other than operate a lathe when you grow up, you would probably have to go somewhere else to live. The mayor of Maidan is the de facto organizer of the lathe operators.

Pyotr Fyodorov's father had worked as a lathe operator at home, but Pyotr remembers accompanying him to the factory about thirty years ago, when his father would bring in the blanks that he had turned. In exchange for the blanks, his father received his salary. Pyotr's mother was also a woodworker: she made whistles.

In Pyotr's backyard are large piles of drying linden logs. Pyotr says that it is best to dry logs vertically so that they dry more evenly, but it is easier to dry them horizontally, which is what he does. He piles them loosely to allow good air circulation and keeps them covered so that moisture will not get in.

The Maidan matryoshki, which are almost always painted by the wives and daughters of the lathe operators, are particularly simple. Most Maidan dolls feature pink circles on their cheeks representing rouge and they usually have one or two big roses in the middle, although these are sometimes replaced by strawberries. In general, because of their lack of detail, Maidan dolls are among the least expensive of all matryoshki.

The majority of the Maidan blanks go to Moscow and from there to Sergiev Posad. On Tuesdays, many of the Maidan wives load bags full of blanks and painted dolls into a bus for the trip to Moscow and the market at Izmailovo. Somehow, they manage to get these bags – which must weight 50 to 100 pounds apiece – to the bus in Maidan and then from the bus to the booth

where they sell their wares. This trip takes eight hours by car and at least twelve hours by bus.

## SEMYONOV

The city of Semyonov is the home of the most common and perhaps the best known style of matryoshka doll to foreigners, because of its large production during the Soviet period. Semyonov, with two matryoshka factories, Khokhlomskaya Rospis (Khokhloma Painting) and Semyonovskaya Rospis (Semyonov Painting) has maintained its position as one of Russia's major producers of the dolls; each factory now produces about 10,000 matryoshki a month. Like Maidan, Semyonov is located in the Nizhny Novgorod oblast. However, it is north of the Volga River, while Maidan is to the south.

In addition to the lathe operators who turn blanks manually, the two Semyonov factories have several automatic lathes made in Germany in the 1970s. These automatic lathes churn out blanks every few seconds for small 3-piece and 4-piece dolls made from the harder, but more brittle birch wood.

*Plate: 217 (above)*
*City: Semyonov*
*The city of Semyonov lies in a shallow valley on the broad plains of western Russia, affording a good view to those who drive in from the south, from Nizhny Novgorod.*

*Plate: 218 (left)*
*Factory: Semyonovskaya Rospis, Semyonov*
*Size: 18-piece, 12 inches tall*
*One of the more impressive traditional Semyonov dolls, this doll is not only larger but much more detailed than most traditional dolls.*

*Plate: 219*
*Factory: Khokhlomskaya Rospis, Semyonov*
*The Khokhlomskaya Rospis factory gate features a monogram of the first letters of the plant's name and a sign proclaiming that its spoons have been made for 1000 years.*

## Khokhlomskaya Rospis

Khokhlomskaya Rospis, which produces matryoshki as well as the traditional Khokhloma wooden bowls and spoons, has more employees than any of the other matryoshka factories. It is a sprawling factory, with several two-story buildings, approximately 25 lathe operators, and 100 artists painting the traditional yellow Semyonov dolls.

In one of the buildings, the Khokhloma style spoons and bowls are also produced. The distinctive Khokhloma style features a gold background with black designs on it, often highlighted by red or orange berries or borders. Production is mostly small jam spoons or soup spoons and bowls, but also includes large bowls featuring a carved head of a swan, some almost two feet in diameter.

Next to the factory is the company store. It displays a modest selection of matryoshki and the gilded Khokhloma products. The store attracts local residents and, as a well established institution of popular culture, also brings Russians from considerable distances to buy the factory's decorative home and kitchen items. The products are purchased for resale, personal use, or, quite frequently, as gifts.

*Plate: 220 (left)*
*Factory: Khokhlomskaya Rospis, Semyonov*
*The woodworking room at the Khokhlomskaya Rospis factory is probably the largest in Russia.*

*Plate: 221 (below)*
*Factory: Khokhlomskaya Rospis, Semyonov*
*The rough lathes are connected to a vacuum system that removes sawdust and wood shavings. The system has not been working for some time, however.*

*Plate: 222 (bottom)*
*Factory: Khokhlomskaya Rospis, Semyonov*
*Collection: Gail Buyske*
*The famous gold tinted spoons, reputedly made in this region for a thousand years.*

*Plate: 223 (below)*
*Factory: Khokhlomskaya Rospis, Semyonov*
*The matryoshka painting room at Khokhlomskaya Rospis is large and open. Here, artists consult with the art director about a detail of a doll.*

*Plate: 224 (above)*
*Factory: Semyonovskaya Rospis, Semyonov*
*The Semyonovskaya Rospis factory gate is decorated with a painting of a matryoshka doll on sheet metal.*

*Plate: 225 (left)*
*Factory: Semyonovskaya Rospis, Semyonov*
*Nataliya Sergeevna, the art director at Semyonovskaya Rospis, oversees the artists at the factory and is also responsible for introducing new designs into production.*

## Semyonovskaya Rospis

The Semyonovskaya Rospis factory is similar to its cross-town rival, except that it concentrates on matryoshki. Like almost all of the matryoshka factories in Russia, it features a metal gate with a matryoshka emblem attached. The Semyonovskaya Rospis factory is built vertically, with the artists on the third floor and the lacquer room on the fourth.

While both of the Semyonov factories produce thousands of the yellow Semyonov dolls, they are both trying to produce more artistically interesting doll as well. The art director at Semyonovskaya Rospis, Nataliya Sergeevna Bakharyova, is therefore responsible both for ensuring that the yellow dolls

are being painted correctly and for introducing new designs into production. Nataliya is developing a new artistic section in the factory, where the artists create their own designs. Some of these will be reproduced on the factory floor, while some will be sold as one-of-a-kind dolls.

## Kirov

The Kirov factory is the single largest matryoshka factory in Russia and employs the most matryoshka artists. The city of Kirov itself is a large, bustling city located on a bend in the Vyatka River, which flows north and west around the city and then south into the Volga. Because of its location on a Volga tributary, it has historically been a trading city. Like Nizhny Novgorod *oblast,* Kirov *oblast* is known for its master woodworkers and toy makers. The Kirov matryoshka factory, founded in the early 1930s, is located in the southern part of Kirov, in what used to be a small village but has now been absorbed into the city.

*Plate: 226, 227 (above, below)*
*Factory: Art Alliance, Kirov*
*The Kirov factory is an impressively large facility with a small office building at the gate (below). Outside the main factory building (above), logs are stored. The logs are squared in the factory mill, with the ends rounded to be fit into the chuck of the lathe.*

*Plate: 228*
*Factory: Art Alliance, Kirov*
*The logs are brought into the building on a mechanized conveyor system and fed into a saw that removes the bark. Here, we see birch logs, easily identifiable by their light, striated bark.*

The Kirov factory is the home of matryoshki with straw designs. This innovation was introduced in the 1960s and was one of the few changes in matryoshka design in the 60 years that production was controlled by the Soviet government. It was adapted from the Kirov tradition of wooden boxes decorated with straw.

The straw starts out as long, thin stalks. The women who work with the straw, who are all in one room together, make a cut down one side of the stalks, then pull them against knives held on a cutting board, turning the stalks into flat strips. Then they use tools to cut the straw into various shapes, depending on what is to be glued onto the doll—diamonds, squares, or curved shapes that will form a geometric design or perhaps a flower.

However, the straw design dolls are only a small part of the factory's output; the Kirov factory is the only one in Russia that has not limited itself to its local matryoshka traditions. It produces a wide variety of matryoshki, some of which are in the style of other Russian regions. Some critics believe that the factory should maintain the regional traditions, while its supporters praise it for its business-like approach.

The Kirov factory is business-like in other ways as well; the factory has its own sawmill. While other factories process wood from timber, the Kirov factory's mill, which includes heavy

conveyor and cutting equipment, efficiently handles the logs, strips the bark off the logs, and cuts them into workpieces. The logs are cut into squares about four by four inches in section, and 24 inches long. A rough lathe cuts a rounded end to fit the chucks of the fine-turning lathes. The logs are stored for further curing or as inventory before being taken to the lathe room to be shaped into dolls.

The factory is expanding its output and most of the over 200 artists, which, unusually, include a few men, are graduates from the local art school. They are paid a relatively high starting wage, especially for artists in a provincial city, and are expected to produce efficiently.

The Kirov factory's owner, Andrei Kouleshov, can claim responsibility for this expansion trend. Like many Russian factories, the Kirov matryoshka factory was privatized in the early 1990s and each of the employees received a share. Andrei spent a year convincing the employees that it was in their best interest to sell him their shares, until eventually he accumulated a controlling interest in the factory. The Kirov factory, now called Art Alliance, is one of the very few factories of any kind in Kirov that is actually expanding in new equipment and added jobs. Distribution and marketing were also given new life. Since this is certainly one of only a few matryoshka factories that seems to be thriving, it appears that the employees made the right choice.

*Plate: 229*
*Factory: Art Alliance, Kirov*
*These dolls, taken from crates of inventory, are being inspected for improper fit or other deformities, before being batched in large trays and sent to be primed with starch.*

*Plate: 230 (above)*
*Factory: Art Alliance, Kirov*
*The art studios in Kirov are brightly lit and lively. A job at Art Alliance is prized for good pay and reliable employment.*

*Plate: 231 (right)*
*Factory: Art Alliance, Kirov*
*In this studio room, six large tables make workspace for six to eight artists each.*

Plate: 232 (left)
Factory: Art Alliance, Kirov
Potal is gold or silver foil which is supplied to the factories on a paper backing. The women cut out the desired design, and then use heated blocks to fuse potal to the blank.

Plate: 233 (left)
Factory: Art Alliance, Kirov
The rye straw appliqué technique, for which the Kirov studios are known, begins with whole straw, some of it dyed in bright colors. The straw is slit down the side. It is flattened by pulling it between a sharp tool and a cutting board, creating a straight, narrow strip of long-grained material.

Plate: 234 (left)
Factory: Art Alliance, Kirov
The artist, using a variety of shaped knives or chisels, cuts out shapes that will be used to form flower designs or geometric patterns on the doll. Most of these pieces are quite tiny—less than 0.25 inches long. The knives are wielded with lightning speed and agility.

Plate: 235 (above)
Factory: Art Alliance, Kirov
Regardless of the decorative technique used (paint, straw appliqué, or potal), the same time-tested means of applying lacquer to the dolls is used. In Kirov, there are several women who do this job.

*Plates: 236 (above)*
*and 237 (opposite)*
*Title: Traditional Kirov doll*
*Factory: Art Alliance, Kirov*
*Size: 10-piece, 8 inches tall*
*Artist: factory artists*
*These traditional Kirov dolls are decorated with countless meticulously placed bits of straw.*

*Plate: 238 (above)*
*City: Nolinsk*
*A patched panorama looking north from a hill on the road south of the fertile Nolinsk valley.*

*Plate: 239 (right)*
*City: Nolinsk*
*Near the town square is the art school that has trained many of the artists who now work in the Vyatskii Souvenir factory.*

*Plate: 240 (inset)*
*City: Nolinsk*
*The sign reads: RF (Russian Federation); Kirov oblast (state); SCHOOL OF ART; city of Nolinsk*

## NOLINSK

Nolinsk is approximately 100 miles south of Kirov in the broad Russian farmland. A stream that feeds the Vyatka River runs nearby. The city is like many in rural areas, with a central square dedicated to local men who fought in World War II. Here, however, an art school occupies a building near the square. Many of the school's students find work in the matryoshka trade when they complete their training.

*Plate: 241 (left)*
*Factory: Vyatskii Souvenir, Nolinsk*
*The entrance to the Vyatskii Souvenir factory is an unassuming door next to the factory gate.*

The factory itself, Vyatskii Souvenir, is large, with about 100 artists and another 50 people to prepare the blanks, lacquer the dolls, and take

*Plate: 242 (right)*
*Factory: Vyatskii Souvenir, Nolinsk*
*The pneumatically powered blade of the splitter cuts the log in half. After each half is split at least into quarters, the pieces will go to the rough lathe to be rounded or squared.*

*Plate: 243 (below)*
*Factory: Vyatskii Souvenir, Nolinsk*
*Some of the logs go to the table saw for cutting into square pieces for further curing or storage.*

care of administrative matters. Nolinsk is in the Kirov *oblast* where rye crops are abundant. Therefore its production also includes straw appliqué technique in decorating the dolls. The manufacturing facility is among the least advanced of Russian matryoshka factories, perhaps because of its rural, quite remote location.

*Plate: 244*
*Factory: Vyatskii Souvenir, Nolinsk*
*The rate of production of the blanks does not always equal the output of finished dolls. Completed blanks are stored in crates until the artists are ready to paint them.*

Vyatskii Souvenir occupies three floors, surrounding a courtyard. Men bring the logs into the cutting area on carts. The factory has a very friendly air. The women artists giggle when foreign visitors pass through. Adjacent to the factory is a gift shop that sells the factory's dolls – as well as combs, razor blades, and toothpaste. Retail stores in small cities cannot afford to specialize too much.

*Plate: 245 (above)*
*Factory: Vyatskii Souvenir, Nolinsk*
*At Vyatskii Souvenir, the painting room is long and narrow.*

*Plate: 246*
*Factory: Vyatskii Souvenir, Nolinsk*
*In a room separate from the painting room, women slice open the tubular strands of straw, some of which is dyed, flatten it, and cut it into various shapes. These shapes will be applied to create flowers or other patterns on the dolls.*

*Plate: 247 (above)*
*Title: Matryoshka with Straw*
*Factory: Vyatskii Souvenir, Nolinsk*
*Artist: factory artists*
*Size: 3-piece, 2.7 inches tall*
*This small doll is enlarged to show the straw appliqué. The last piece does not have much detail, but it does have one little straw flower.*

*Plate: 248 (left)*
*Factory: Vyatskii Souvenir, Nolinsk*
*The artists use either a small blade or a needle-like instrument to put the straw into place, and then a brush to apply the glue that will infuse the straw and stick it to the doll.*

ВТОРАЯ
25Р
ВТОРАЯ

*Plate: 249 (opposite, above)*
*Factory: Vyatskii Souvenir, Nolinsk*
*After the dolls are painted and lacquered, they are taken to the warehouse, where they await shippers, or visitors who come to purchase them.*

*Plate: 250 (opposite, below)*
*Factory: Vyatskii Souvenir, Nolinsk*
*Although Nolinsk is a long trip for big city or foreign visitors, the factory store is well stocked with matryoshki and other products from the factory, such as Christmas ornaments.*

*Plate: 251 (left)*
*Title: Matryoshka with Straw*
*Factory: Vyatskii Souvenir, Nolinsk*
*Artist: factory artists*
*Size: 6-piece, 4.5 inches tall*
*This is the typical color combination of Nolinsk nesting dolls. This model comes in a variety of sizes, ranging from three to twenty pieces, and sometimes more.*

*Plate: 252 (opposite)*
*Title: Mari-El doll*
*City: Yoshkar-Ola*
*Artist: Pavlycheva*
*Size: 7-piece, 6 inches tall*
*This doll portrays a typical Yoshkar-Ola native wearing a traditional costume. The doll is much more detailed than the souvenir dolls that were produced in the now defunct Yoshkar-Ola factory.*

## Yoshkar-Ola

The Yoshkar-Ola factory is mentioned in the books by Larisa Soloviova (see Bibliography), and my collection includes one matryoshka made there in the 1970s. The city of Yoshkar-Ola is about a six-hour drive from Kirov, in the Republic of Mari-El, which in Soviet times was called the Mari-El Autonomous Republic. It is one of several republics along the Volga River that was settled by Asians centuries ago.

The Yoshkar-Ola matryoshka factory was apparently purchased in the mid-1990s by a company called Pyorlik, but it has been closed for several years. The only remnants of the factory are a few artists who paint dolls in traditional costume that are sold at a small souvenir shop. Mari-El dolls tend to have Asian characteristics, providing a striking example of how folk artists adapt a handcraft tradition to their environment. One might even wonder whether the survival of these characteristics during the conformist Soviet period was a way for the Mari-El artists to maintain the sense of individuality that has blossomed in all artists since the demise of the Soviet Union.

*Plate: 253 (above)*
*Title: Mari-El doll*
*City: Yoshkar-Ola*
*Artist: M. Shirmanova*
*Size: 3-piece, 6.5 inches tall*
*This doll was produced by an independent artist in Yoshkar-Ola.*

*Plate: 254 (overleaf)*
*City: Yoshkar-Ola*
*Artist: factory artists*
*Size: 9-piece, 5 inches tall*
*Collection: Rett and Tania Ertl*
*This doll was made in the Soviet Union in the 1970s. The factory no longer operates. The doll's small size, large number of pieces, and Asian look were an unusual combination for the Soviet period.*

# Entrepreneurs in the New Russia

33
ПРОВАНСАЛЬ

# The Artists
# Entrepreneurs in the New Russia

Matryoshka artists have unique accounts of how they adopted their profession, and correspondingly unique styles. Because the rebirth of matryoshka art resulted from the demise of the Soviet system, many of today's artists turned to matryoshka painting as a way to make ends meet, or as a way to fulfill artistic leanings that they could not pursue in the planned economy. The artists featured in this chapter are all individuals with whom TolsToys has had the pleasure of working over the years. They all paint independently, in their own homes or studios, and were deliberately selected to represent various types and styles of dolls, from various locations. Some of these artists are professionally trained; most are self-taught. Some paint expensive, unique dolls, and produce as few as one or two a week; others are prolific and paint as many as 100 dolls per week.

Unfortunately, not all independently-minded artists have survived Russia's transition to a market economy. One such artist is Irina Afonina, who painted under the pseudonym Marfa. The distinctive faces of Marfa's matryoshki reflect her training at the Sergiev Posad School of Icon Painting, and the scenes that she painted on the stomachs—churches, *troikas,* and even a portrait of poet Alexander Pushkin—are works of art. But even though her nesting dolls are of high quality and are relatively expensive, Marfa has taken a job painting trays in a factory.

*Plate: 255 (chapter title)*
*City: Orekhovo-Zuyevo*
*Dolls drying in Sergei Koblov's workshop.*

*Plate: 256 (opposite)*
*City: Sergiev Posad*
*A tabletop is also a palette in Zhanna Nikolaeva's home.*

*Plate: 257 (below)*
*Title: Troika*
*Artist: Marfa (I. Afonina)s*
*Size: 10-piece, 10.5 inches tall*
*Collection: Vicki Miller*
*Marfa, who studied at the Sergiev Posad School of Icon Painting, has stopped painting matryoshki.*

## Natasha Grigorieva

Natasha Grigorieva lives in Krasnozavodsk, a city formerly dominated by a major ammunition factory, which is located just north of Sergiev Posad. (Ironically, this factory has produced a number of matryoshka artists.) Natasha was born in the Russian north; like many Russians, she studied hard so that she could leave her village. She was admitted to the Institute of Aviation Instrument Manufacture in St. Petersburg and, after graduation, was assigned to the Krasnozavodsk factory as a quality control specialist. Natasha started matryoshka painting as a hobby in 1990, influenced by her proximity to Sergiev Posad. She left her job in 1992 and was soon making more money selling matryoshki than she had at the factory, which by that time was reducing staff.

Natasha's matryoshki are quite simple, but have two endearing features: their faces and their colors. Natasha's blue-eyed faces are truly charming and win the hearts of many beginning collectors. Natasha's dolls also feature contemporary colors including lime green, pink, navy blue, forest green, purple, burgundy, and deep red (as opposed to the orange-red favored by the factories), and, unusually but effectively, black. Natasha paints the background just one color: the scarf and apron, for example, are maroon, as is the base of the doll.

Natasha, who is self-taught, is an especially dedicated artist. She paints from eight to twelve hours per day, five days a week. She specializes

*Plate: 258 (above, top)*
*City: Sergiev Posad*
*Natasha Grigorieva is one of many artists who used to make a living at the ammunition factory at Krasnozavodsk.*

*Plate: 259 (above, bottom)*
*City: Sergiev Posad*
*Natasha dries her dolls on spikes poked into a large piece of Styrofoam.*

*Plate: 260 (right)*
*City: Sergiev Posad*
*Artist: Natasha Grigorieva*
*Size: 5-piece, 4 inches tall*

in 10-piece pot-bellied dolls, but also paints 5-piece minimats, 5-piece "classicals," as well as some 7-piece dolls. Natasha can make ten 10-piece dolls per week and as many as thirty 5-piece dolls.

Like many other artists, Natasha sells her dolls at the Izmailovo market in Moscow. Although she now has enough standing orders that she can work without making the trek to Moscow every week, she still buys all of her materials at Izmailovo: gouache paint, bronze watercolor, and Turkish lacquer. Natasha uses a squirrel-hair brush for the background of her dolls, and kolinsky (an Asian mink) for the fine brushwork. A squirrel brush lasts for three weeks; she has to change kolinsky brushes every week.

Natasha is also an entrepreneur. She has gathered a small group that specializes in simpler dolls and that can produce several hundred dolls per month. Among the dolls that they have produced is a 3-piece wedding party favor based on an original produced by Igor Gumnitsky in St. Petersburg.

Divorced, Natasha lives in Krasnozavodsk with her teenage son, Zhenya. She is putting her son through tourism school, but he also enjoys painting from time to time.

## Lyudmila and Aleksei Kremnev

Lyuda (Lyudmila) and Aleksei were both born in Sergiev Posad in the 1960s; they married each other in 1988. Aleksei worked as a plumber

*Plate: 261 (left)*
*City: Sergiev Posad*
*Lyuda holds one of the Kremnevs' most popular dolls, a tiny penguin in a top hat.*

*Plate: 262 (below)*
*City: Sergiev Posad*
*Lyuda measuring and marking the area for the face of a minimat.*

*Plate: 263 (below)*
*Title: Micro Girl 3-piece*
*City: Sergiev Posad*
*Artist: L. and A. Kremnev*
*Size: 3-piece, 0.8 inches tall*

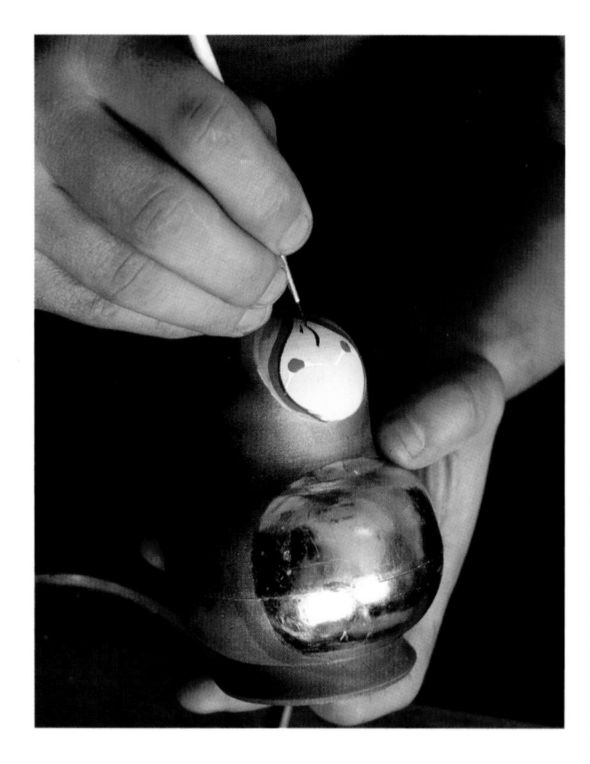

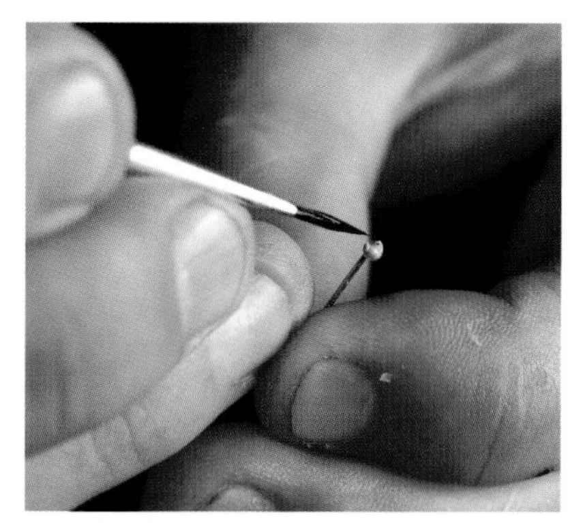

*Plate: 264 (above)*
*City: Sergiev Posad*
*The minimat is a large surface, practically a mural for Alexei.*

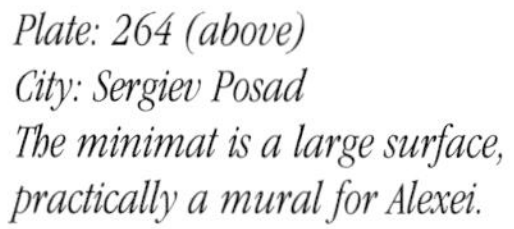

*Plate: 265 (above, right)*
*City: Sergiev Posad*
*Even the larger pieces of micro-mats are too small to hold between Alexei's fingers, so he sticks them on the end of a discarded syringe.*

*Plate: 266 (right)*
*City: Sergiev Posad*
*The Kremnevs' coffee table doubles as a work table.*

and janitor in a Sergiev Posad factory until 1991, while Lyuda worked as a cook. They knew that the matryoshka business was providing a living for several of their fellow citizens, so, when the factory had trouble paying salaries, they decided to give matryoshki a try. Lyuda and Aleksei are both self-taught, although they both enjoyed their art classes from their school days. They sold their first matryoshka for 180 rubles, which at the time was the same amount as Aleksei's monthly salary at the factory.

Lyuda and Aleksei specialize in micromats,

usually of 3, 5, 7, or 10 pieces. The 3-piece micros are only about a half-inch high, while the smallest piece of the 10-piece is barely an eighth of an inch high. Lyuda and Aleksei work with one lathe operator in Maidan, who produces the tiny blanks for them. Their matryoshki feature sweet faces that change from piece to piece; the first one may have a whimsical smile, the second a big wink, and the third a look of surprise. They are also the authors of one of the most popular micros—penguins, either purple or black.

Lyuda and Aleksei work together; she paints the background and the flowers and also does the potal work. Aleksei paints the faces and the fine details. Their paints are gouache and acrylic. Their brushes are made from kolinsky and squirrel hair.

Lyuda and Aleksei work hard —twelve hours a day, five days a week, although Lyuda also enjoys working around the house. In the winter they work in their apartment; in the summer, they work on their open-air balcony. They also take a month off in the summer. On Wednesdays, they sell their wares at wholesale day at the Izmailovo market. Aleksei would rather work at the factory where he worked for many years, but like many factories, there is no work there now.

*Plate: 267 (above)*
*City: Sergiev Posad*
*Zhanna Nikolaeva uses egg whites to prime the blanks, rather than the starch used in most factories.*

*Plate: 268 (left)*
*Title: Mother and Child*
*City: Sergiev Posad*
*Artist: Zhanna Nikolaeva*
*Size: 10-piece, 10 inches tall*
*Collection: Vicki Miller*
*Zhanna Nikolaeva's painting of quilts is indicative of the work that goes into every one of her matryoshki.*

## Zhanna Nikolaeva

Zhanna was born in 1964 in Murom, just an hour's drive from the village of Maidan. In 1985 she graduated from the University at Nizhny Novgorod with a degree in mathematics and programming and was assigned to a job as a programmer in Sergiev Posad. Zhanna painted her first matryoshka in 1991 under the tutelage of her older sister,

*Plate: 269*
*Title: Bread and Salt*
*City: Sergiev Posad*
*Artist: Zhanna Nikolaeva*
*Size: 5-piece, 4 inches tall*
*Bread and salt are symbols of hospitality not only in Russian culture, but throughout most Caucasus and Central Asian countries of the former Soviet Union.*

who is a professional artist. Zhanna started with biblical subjects and experimented with matryoshki painted in the style of lacquer boxes from Palekh and Mstyora. In 1993, she designed her signature "Nikolaeva" doll.

Zhanna's trademark dolls depict a peasant woman holding a baby wrapped in a patchwork quilt. She uses bright primary colors: blue, red, and green, and a lot of white. Her paints are watercolors, temperas, and acrylics. Egg white is used as primer.

Zhanna tried to work with a group of colleagues, hiring people to paint the background colors and other less complex features of the dolls, but she was always unsatisfied with the results. Now she works alone. Her two teenaged children help her by sanding and priming the blanks. Zhanna works sixteen hours a day, six days a week— sometimes even seven. Zhanna spends weekends at the Izmailovo market, but most of her work goes toward filling special orders. She takes ten days off every year, usually in her hometown of Murom. Zhanna has visited Turkey and was invited to Switzerland to demonstrate the craft of matryoshka making.

## Natasha Minenko

Natasha was born in 1958 in the village of Khotkovo. She loved art as a child, but never pursued it as a career. From 1979 until 1993, Natasha worked as a maître d' at the Izmailovo Hotel. Because the hotel was near the Izmailovo market and because Natasha lived near Sergiev Posad, the idea of becoming an artist blossomed with the collapse of the Soviet Union. Natasha started by taking lessons from her friends and neighbors, copying others' matryoshki. Soon she was selling her matryoshki to a cooperative group that was reselling them. Finally, Natasha quit her job and started painting full time, selling her dolls on wholesale day at the Izmailovo market.

Natasha specializes in small, 5-piece potbellied girls with angelic faces, Santas with red cheeks, and peasant grandmothers with families. She especially enjoys painting faces.

Natasha works alone, up to fourteen hours a day, four to six days per week. She is very prolific, producing up to twenty-five 5-piece dolls per day. She no longer spends much time at Izmailovo, as she receives orders on a regular basis. Natasha takes three weeks off in the summer, often driving her own car to her dacha, which is 30 miles from her Khotkovo apartment.

Natasha's husband, Vasilii Nikolaevich, works in construction, and after work he participates in the family business, lacquering Natasha's dolls. Her son, Roman, works as a driver for a Japanese company and has moved out of the family apartment. Natasha's daughter, Irina, occasionally helps her paint matryoshki.

*Plate: 270 (above)*
*City: Orekhovo-Zuyevo*
*Sergei Koblov is one of the few artists who carves his designs in nesting dolls.*

*Plate: 271 (left)*
*Title: Santa mini*
*City: Khotkovo*
*Artist: Natasha Minenko*
*Size: 5-piece, 4 inches tall*
*A rosy-cheeked Santa in the minimat format.*

## Sergei Koblov

Sergei Koblov was born and grew up near Orekhovo-Zuyevo, a half hour's drive east of Moscow. He graduated from the prestigious Bauman Higher Technical School in Moscow as an electrical engineer. Unable to find work after graduation, Sergei remembered how his father had taught him to carve, so he returned home to try to make a living using his childhood hobby. He began to carve and paint a series of designs.

Sergei's matryoshki are some of the most original in Russia. There are a few other artists who carve matryoshki, but most of them carve only superficially, adding lines to beards or faces. Sergei carves the actual figures into the wood, thereby creating a completely different effect. Sergei specializes in traditional folk tales. Among

his best dolls is *The Turnip*, described in Chapter 4, which pictures each of the characters of the story pulling on the shirttail of the next one. The pièce de résistance is the innermost piece, which is a little carved turnip. Sergei has also developed dolls for a series of tales, including *The Kolobok, The Teremok, Masha and the Bear,* and *The Spotted Hen*. In addition, Sergei does several different religious dolls: a series of saints, Noah's ark, Life of Christ, and Nativity.

Like many folk artists, Sergei is proud of his techniques. He makes his own carving tools and his own paints, which are completely nontoxic and harmless to the environment. Sergei uses ancient recipes to make his paints and will not divulge the ingredients or the methods that he uses to prepare them.

*Plate: 272 (above, left)*
*City: Orekhovo-Zuyevo*
*Sergei Koblov painting in his workshop.*

*Plate: 273 (below)*
*Title: Musicians*
*City: Orekhovo-Zuyevo*
*Artist: S. Koblov*
*Size: 5-piece, 6.5 inches tall*
*An example of Sergei Koblov's creativity, this family of musicians is punctuated by the baby singing along as the smallest piece.*

Sergei has organized a studio at the House of Culture in Davydovo; the studio is important for him as a way to contribute to the community. The participants are mostly students and housewives, ranging in age from eighteen to fifty. Sergei gives them lessons, provides them a place to work, and, perhaps most important, sells their work in Moscow. He does not charge the pupils for the lessons, but does make a small profit on sales.

## Natasha Pugaeva

Natasha Pugaeva grew up in Sergiev Posad, where she attended art school. Natasha spent a year at the Institute of Energetics in Moscow, where she met her future husband. The couple moved to Kazakhstan, where Natasha taught painting and tried her hand at painting on wood.

*Plate: 274 (above)*
*City: Raduzhnoye*
*Natasha Pugaeva puts the finishing touches on her Santa doll.*

*Plate: 275 (left)*
*Title: Dunya*
*City: Raduzhnoye*
*Artist: N. Pugaeva*
*Size: 5-piece, 6 inches tall*
*Natasha Pugaeva gives her simple dolls the peasant name Dunya.*

ТУШЕНКА
М.

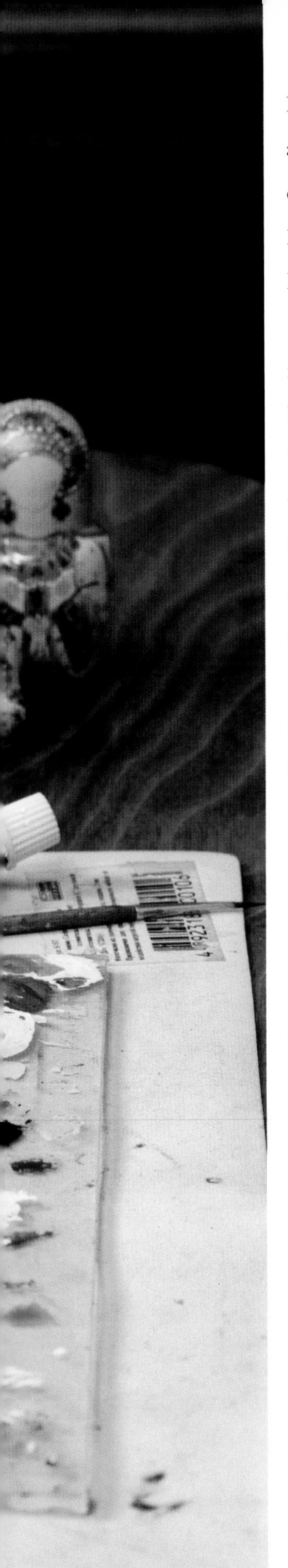

In 1990 she painted her first matryoshka. Natasha and her husband moved to Raduzhnoye, a small city about 120 miles east of Moscow, in 1993. Natasha quit teaching at that point and devoted herself full time to painting matryoshki.

Natasha produces some of the finest matryoshki in Russia. Her work is characterized by *potal,* haunting faces, detailed paintings, and little spots of sparkle that represent gems. She is a versatile artist; her themes range from whimsical folk tales (*The Turnip*) and fairy tales (*Emelya and the Pike*) to religious subjects and even scenes of ancient Rome.

Natasha opened a studio in 1995. Her ten students paint, and she makes corrections, adds finishing touches, and then paints the most difficult parts—the faces and miniatures. Natasha's students do not pay for the lessons, and she pays them part of the revenue from sales. Two of her students, who are described below, have gone out on their own and now sell their matryoshki independently: her mother-in-law, Irina Petrovna Balashova, and her older sister Valya Evdokimova. Natasha works twelve hours a day, three days a week at home and two days a week in the studio. On weekends, she takes the train to the Izmailovo market, where she meets new customers. However, most of Natasha's work comes from existing customers. As a reliable source of the highest quality work, she often has work ordered far in advance for both herself and her students in the matryoshka trade.

*Plate: 276 (left)*
*City: Raduzhnoye*
*Natasha Pugaeva's work table, with ornately dressed dolls and Santas in progress, is as neat and well controlled as her painting.*

*Plate: 277 (below)*
*Title: Princess Olga*
*City: Raduzhnoye*
*Artist: I. Balashova*
*Size: 5-piece, 6 inches tall*
*Collection: Vicki Miller*
*Irina Balashova, Natasha Pugaeva's mother-in-law, names her matryoshki after historical characters – in this case, the first recorded female ruler in Russia, and the first member of the ruling family of Kiev to adopt Christianity.*

*Plate: 278 (overleaf, left page)*
*Title: Life of Christ*
*City: Raduzhnoye*
*Artist: N. Pugaeva*
*Size: 10-piece, 10 inches tall*
*Collection: Vicki Miller*

*Plate: 279 (overleaf, right page)*
*Title: Life of Christ*
*City: Raduzhnoye*
*Artist: N. Pugaeva*
*Size: 5-piece, 6 inches tall*
*Collection: Vicki Miller*
*Natasha Pugaeva paints a variety of religious dolls depicting scenes from the life of Christ.*

## Irina Balashova

Irina was born in Kazakhstan in 1947 and moved to Raduzhnoye in 1991. She was trained as a mathematician and has done some computer programming. Until 1996, she was a math teacher. Irina painted her first doll in 1991, with encouragement from her daughter-in-law, Natasha. In 1996 Irina left her teaching job, where her pay was very low, and began to make her living on matryoshki.

Irina's matryoshki feature bright colors and many gem-like sparkles. Many of them represent tsarevnas and princesses from Russian history, often clad in fur or fancy throws. She uses a variety of paints, including water colors, gouache, tempera, and "metallic" acrylics.

Irina worked on her own for the first four

*Plate: 280 (above)*
*City: Raduzhnoye*
*Irina Balashova at work.*

*Plate: 281 (right)*
*City: Raduzhnoye*
*A family portrait – Natasha Pugaeva, her son Dima, her mother-in-law Irina Balashova, and her sister Valya Evdokimova.*

years. Now she usually works in a team of four people; they sand the blanks, help Irina paint the background colors, apply the *potal,* and sometimes paint the outlines on the dolls. Irina designs her own matryoshki and paints all of the detail work herself, while her husband, Vyacheslav, lacquers her dolls. Irina tries to work 12 hours a day three days a week and several hours a day on two other days. On weekends, she sells her dolls at Izmailovo. Irina also displays her work in various salons and stores in Moscow.

## Valya Evdokimova

Valya was born in Sergiev Posad in 1970. She graduated from the Institute of Energetics in Moscow, and worked as an engineer in Zagorsk until 1991.

Valya has loved to paint since childhood. She spent a year at art school, and became proficient at painting portraits. She painted her first matryoshka in 1991. Valya first worked and studied with her sister Natasha Pugaeva, before becoming an independent artist.

Valya's matryoshki feature lace-like details and carefully crafted faces. Many of her dolls have religious overtones. One of her favorite pieces is a *nevalyashka* with a portrait. Valya uses *potal* and sparkles sparingly, thereby giving her dolls a refined feel.

Valya spends more than 40 hours a week painting matryoshki, but takes a month off every year. She usually spends her vacations with her sister Natasha in Raduzhnoye, but one summer she was able to visit Rome. Valya has a daughter, Masha, who is studying ballet and also likes to paint. Though Masha has painted on matryoshka blanks, it may be a while before she joins the business with her mother.

*Plate: 282 (above)*
*City: Raduzhnoye*
*Valya Evdokimova studied art for a year, but was convinced to paint matryoshki by her sister, Natasha.*

*Plate: 283 (left)*
*Title: Portraits*
*City: Sergiev Posad*
*Artist: Valya Evdokimova*
*Valya's portraits resemble women carrying icons.*

*Plate: 284 (opposite)*
*City: Raduzhnoye*
*Irina Balashova uses a pencil to outline the features on the face of one of her princesses.*

*Plate: 285 (left)*
*City: Raduzhnoye*
*Artist: I. Balashova*
*Size: 5-piece, 6 inches tall*
*Irina Balashova specializes in 19th-century ladies wearing jewelry and sequined clothing.*

*Plate: 286 (above)*
*Title: Portrait*
*City: Sergiev Posad*
*Artist: V. Evdokimova*
*Size: 1-piece* nevalyashka, *4.5 inches tall*
*Like her portrait matryoshki, Valya Evdokimova's* nevalyashki *have religious overtones.*

*Plate: 287 (above)*
*City: St. Petersburg*
*Marina Andrianova prefers to do original matryoshki, rather than producing several copies of the same doll.*

*Plate: 288 (opposite)*
*City: St. Petersburg*
*Still life with Marina's glasses.*

*Plate: 289 (opposite, inset)*
*City: St. Petersburg*
*Marina paints details on the face of a matryoshka.*

## Marina Andrianova

Marina was born in 1958 in Estonia. She graduated from the Herzen Teaching Institute with a major in graphic arts and became an art teacher, including teaching for 14 years at the Gorky House of Culture in St. Petersburg. Like so many other artists, Marina painted her first matryoshka in 1991. Her first matryoshki were copies, but soon she began to create her own designs.

Marina's matryoshki are unusual. She typically paints details all over the doll, often using translucent paint. Her subjects include country scenes, featuring summer and winter landscapes, and depicting fences as well as birds, cats, and other animals. Marina likes to use the wood grain of the matryoshka in her painting.

Most of all, Marina enjoys designing her own matryoshki. She works on her matryoshki for three or four hours a day and paints year-round; in the summertime she paints at her dacha. She often works in a team, in which case she paints the miniatures and landscapes. Marina can paint 10 miniatures or one entire 10-piece matryoshka in an evening. Unlike most artists, perhaps because she lives in St. Petersburg, Marina does not sell her own matryoshki, but instead sells them to wholesalers.

Marina's husband, Alexei, is also an artist. Their daughter, Nadezhda, is pursuing an education in the humanities with an emphasis on English language studies.

*Plate: 290 (left)*
*City: St. Petersburg*
*Svetlana Ruts and her husband Igor Gumnitsky paint dolls in their home. Igor maintains a separate studio where he pursues a career as a fine artist.*

*Plate: 291 (below)*
*City: St. Petersburg*
*Like other painters, Svetlana and Igor devote a very small area of their home, just this desk, for matryoshka painting.*

## Igor Gumnitsky

Igor was born in 1944 and graduated from the prestigious Leningrad Repin Art Academy in 1971. Since then, he has taught painting at that institution, which is now called the St. Petersburg Academy of Art. Igor painted his first matryoshka in 1987. He did not paint it for commercial reasons but rather out of intellectual curiosity; he liked the shape of the matryoshka, and he wanted to try something different. Igor works in tandem with his wife, Svetlana, who was his student at the academy. She usually paints the fine details, and Igor paints the rest.

Igor is a matryoshka designer and has developed a series called "professionals": doctor, dentist, teacher, nanny, and chef. One of his favorite dolls is the "casino man," which depicts a gambler who slowly loses his shirt—and everything else. Igor also designed a matryoshka based on the fairy tale *The Mistress of Copper Mountain* by Pavel Bazhov. His trademarks are distinct lines and rich colors.

Igor and Svetlana sell their matryoshki to wholesale companies and occasionally receive special orders. Igor works on matryoshki for two or three hours a day. He has a studio, where he does most of his painting—on canvas. Matryoshka painting is a sideline for him, and he does it at home. They spend their holidays at the dacha, where Igor continues to work.

Igor and Svetlana have a son, Radislav, who attends the Art Lyceum of the Repin Art Academy. Radislav helps his parents by painting backgrounds. It is not just the next generation of matryoshka lovers that is emerging now; it is also the next generation of artists.

*Plate: 292*
*Title: Casino Guy*
*City: St. Petersburg*
*Artist: I. Gumnitsky*
*Size: 5-piece, 6 inches tall*
*This is not a traditional Russian folk tale, but certainly a tale too often told. The gambler has lost his shirt. And more. One of the wedding party dolls by Gumnitsky can be seen in Chapter 4.*

*Plate: 293 (above)*
*Title: Noah's Ark*
*City: Orekhovo-Zuyevo*
*Artist: Sergei Koblov*
*Size: 5-piece, 6.5 inches tall*
*Collection: John and Tracy Hausman*

*One of Sergei Koblov's most popular themes, featuring his trademark bas relief technique to depict several of the animals from Noah's ark. He accents his carving with the use of vegetable dyes and shading techniques to emphasize the most important parts of the doll.*

*Plate: 294 (opposite)*
*Title: Boyar Family*
*City: Sergiev Posad*
*Artist: D.M. Pichugin*
*Size: 10-piece, 8.5 inches tall*
*Collection: Artistic-Pedagogical Museum of Toys*
*An early matryoshka painted by a member of one of the best known families of artists. (Early 1900s)*

# 7 Collecting Matryoshki
## One is Never Enough

## Collecting Matryoshki

# One is Never Enough

COLLECTING MATRYOSHKI is a relatively new endeavour, because new and interesting matryoshki have only been introduced since the late 1980s. Therefore a collector starting now can still be a pioneer and collect work by artists whose reputations are only beginning to develop. Furthermore, matryoshki are still relatively affordable, considering the individual effort that goes into making each doll. As a result, matryoshka collecting is an accessible and fascinating way to participate personally in the re-birth of a Russian folk art tradition.

## Approaches to Collecting

The first rule of collecting art applies also to matryoshki—if you like a doll and can afford it, buy it. Just as tastes vary in art, so they vary in matryoshka dolls.

A beginning collector might want to have one doll from each of the regions of Russia—Sergiev Posad, Maidan, Semyonov, Kirov, and Nolinsk. These dolls can be relatively inexpensive, and you can vary your collection by buying different sizes—say, a 5-piece Sergiev Posad, a 6-piece Semyonov, a 7-piece Nolinsk, a 10-piece Kirov, and a 15-piece Maidan. Many foreigners have a matryoshka that was brought to them from Russia, usually a Semyonov doll. That can serve as the starting point for the collection.

You may then want to expand into the myriad dolls that have appeared since the late 1980s. You may just want to buy dolls that you like, or you may want to focus your collection on a particular theme, type, or even artist.

One thematic approach is to collect dolls depicting as many different folk or fairy tales as possible, or just to collect depictions of one particular tale. This book includes photos of five different versions of *The Turnip,* but there are probably thirty others that are being produced by individuals or factories, in addition to many other one-of-a-kind dolls made by independent artists. This approach can engender satisfying opportunities for further collecting, because many of the stories are also depicted on Russian lacquer boxes and in beautifully illustrated children's books.

Some collectors focus on unusual types of matryoshki. You may decide that you want to buy all of the *nevalyashki* (bells) that you can find, or all the grandmothers.

One unusual collection is being created by a

*Plate: 295 (opposite)*
*Title: Cinderella*
*Artist: Ye. Shuslebina*
*Size: 10-piece, 10 inches tall*
Cinderella *is a fairy tale that is as well known in Russia as elsewhere. The complete doll is shown on the following page.*

*Plate: 296 (above)*
*Title: Cinderella*
*Artist: Ye. Shuslebina*
*Size: 10-piece, 10 inches tall*
*This beautifully painted doll richly illustrates the Cinderella story, much loved in Russia.*

*Plate: 297 (opposite)*
*Title: Siryn, the Magic Bird*
*Artist: N. Romenskaya*
*Size: 10-piece, 10 inches tall*
*Reminiscent of the art of Russia's best known fairy tale illustrator, Ivan Bilibin, Nadezhda Romenskaya's* Siryn *is an explosion of color.*

*Plate: 298*
*Title: Thumbellina*
*Artist: Sv. Brudis*
*Size: 5-piece, 6 inches tall*
*Although the fairy tale was written by Hans Christian Andersen,* Thumbellina *is quite a popular theme in Russia.*

woman we know who has been buying dolls for her granddaughter's birthday. For her second birthday, the little girl received a 2-piece doll; for her third, she received a 3-piece doll. She just turned four. Imagine what the collection will be like if the grandmother lives to celebrate her granddaughter's fiftieth birthday!

If you start to focus your collecting, you will soon become familiar with the work of individual artists. Collecting by artist or groups of artists, such as those of the Abramtsevo school, can be another fulfilling approach., because it creates a personal connection in your collecting. (Although, as is discussed in this chapter, this approach is not always possible, because not all artists sign their work.) It can also be satisfying to develop a sense of what sellers typically charge for dolls by your preferred artists, so that you can recognize a particularly good price when you see it, or can watch the changes in the artist's market status as his or her dolls change in price. You will also begin to recognize more unusual work by your preferred artist, in terms of themes or quality.

Whatever approach you take to collecting,

you will undoubtedly find that it assumes a life of its own.

## Evaluating Quality

Knowing which characteristics are key and which defects to avoid also adds to the enjoyment of collecting, because your ability to differentiate between dolls will continue to develop. You can also avoid paying too much for a doll or, if a particular defect is acceptable to you, possibly negotiate a price for a doll that would otherwise be beyond your budget. Remember, though, that one of the appeals of matryoshki is that they are individually made. Each doll is unique and minor flaws reinforce that quality.

A collectible matryoshka should be made with a high quality blank. Unfortunately, some very good artists do not pay enough attention to the blank; this detracts from the quality and value of their dolls. Furthermore, it is not possible to tell whether the wood for the blank has been cured properly. If it has not been, this flaw will only become apparent after several months. Therefore, if you are buying an expensive matryoshka, do what

*Plate: 299*
*Title: The Nutcracker*
*Artist: Sv. Brudis*
*Size: 5-piece, 5 inches tall*
*This doll illustrates what is probably the best known Russian ballet.*

*Plate: 300 (overleaf)*
*Title: Winter Days*
*Artist: Sv. Brudis*
*Size: 10-piece, 10 inches tall*

*Plate: 301 (right)*
*Title: Tale after Tale*
*Artist: E. Saifulmulukov*
*Size: 7-piece, 8 inches tall*

*Plate: 302 (opposite)*
*Title: Lutist*
*Artist: E. Saifulmulukov*
*Size: 7-piece, 8 inches tall*
*The artist's love of music is expressed as a recurrent theme in his painting.*

Plate: 303 (opposite)
*Title: Music and Dances of the 18th Century*
*Artist: T. Shiryaeva*
*Size: 10-piece, 9 inches tall*
*Tatiana Shiryaeva's rendition of 18th-century music and dances evokes the style of the artwork of that period.*

you can to assure yourself that the seller is committed to the quality of the products.

The doll should stand flat on the table. Each top piece should fit snugly into the bottom piece, but it should not take an enormous effort to separate the pieces. As noted earlier, a bad fit is simply not correctible. Any knots in the wood should be very small and on the back of the doll; otherwise, a knot is a serious defect.

Some people worry about the inside lip of the doll, where there may be a chip. This is a minor flaw, since this part of the doll is not visible when the doll is displayed. Similarly, there can sometimes be a small hole in the bottom of the doll. This is also not a serious defect.

The actual shape of the doll varies the most in the medium price range. Not surprisingly, shapes that require special turning on the lathe are more expensive than the standard shapes. The most expensive matryoshki, however, are usually standard shape, with the focus on the artwork.

The quality of the artwork is clearly key and can be discerned in several different ways. Does the most attention seem to be lavished on the outside doll, or is the level of detail consistent throughout? How fine is the detailed work, especially on the part of the dolls that is characteristic for that type, such as the sleeves of the Yoshkar-Ola dolls or the medallions on many of the artistic dolls? You will find it a lot easier to perceive differences in quality by using a magnifying glass. Once you are satisfied with the quality of the doll's featured characteristics, it is also important to look at the other designs, remembering that it is not unusual for different individuals to paint the featured characteristics and the background designs.

An easy question to ask yourself is whether you like the expression on the doll's face. Artists say that their mood is inevitably expressed in the faces of their dolls; once you have looked carefully at a number of dolls by the same artist, you will probably find yourself agreeing.

There are two lacquering techniques, as described in Chapter 2. Higher end dolls should have brush-painted lacquer, which can be perceived in faint brush strokes over the surface. The most common flaws in the alternative, hand-lacquering, are an uneven buildup that can be seen in an irregular sheen, and deposits of lacquer at the connecting seam between the top and bottom of the dolls or in the indentation above the base.

Finally, a word about signatures. Some of the finest dolls that I have seen are unsigned. Usually this is because the sellers do not want buyers to establish direct contact with the artists. If I have the opportunity, I always ask for the artist's signature, because it does add to the value of the doll, in addition to enhancing the pleasure of collecting. If you are building an extensive collection and have relationships with just a few stores and importers, they should be willing to help ensure that at least your most expensive dolls are signed. However, in my own collecting, I do not hesitate to buy a doll that I like even if it is unsigned.

весёлою
рекой,
лиловым
вереск
Незабудки
там
глядятся
в
волны речки
сквозь траву...
И весь день мне
сказки снятся
Сказки счастья
наяву!

*Plate: 304 (opposite)*
*Title: My Palace is the Forest Green*
*Artist: Ya. Bukhareva*
*Size: 5-piece, 6 inches tall*
*Many artists conceive of the doll as a canvas for their creative work, unrestricted by the convention of one figure on each doll, or the back side being an extension of the front.*

*Plate: 305 (left)*
*This is the back side of the outermost doll on the opposite page.*

*Plate: 306 (above)*
*Title: The Legend of the Virgin and the Unicorn*
*Artist: Ye. Semyonova*
*Size: 7-piece, 7 inches tall*

*Plate: 307 (opposite)*
*The same doll as above, by Semyonova, turned to a fuller view of the principal characters.*

## Judging Rarity

The most fertile period for collecting matryoshki is from the time since the demise of the USSR, due to the number and variety of dolls produced since then. Some of the dolls produced at the beginning of that period already have a special quality, because of the sense of artistic freedom that was unleashed at that time and the care that artists took with their work, once they were able to sell independently for the first time.

It can be difficult to find unique matryoshki from this recent period, however; Russia does not have effective copyright protection and artists often copy each other's work. If you have seen the original work, it is not difficult to identify copies made by others. The craftsmanship of the copies is usually considerably lower, as is the price. In addition, however, artists often repeat their own work. This practice is common in handcrafts worldwide; most crafts artists do not have the financial luxury to market only unique works, so they repeat their proven successes. Therefore, while your purchase could be of original work by the artist, it would not necessarily be unique.

Collecting interesting dolls from the Soviet period is substantially more challenging, both because they were mass produced and because individual sales by artists were illegal. Unfortunately, the factory dolls tend to have little or no information on them about when or where they were made. Some of them originally had

*Plate: 308 (above)*
*Title: My Impressions of Renaissance Painting*
*Artist: Ye. Semyonova*
*Size: 7-piece, 9 inches tall*

*Plate: 309 (opposite)*
*Title: Children*
*Artist: Ya. Bubnova*
*Size: 7-piece, 8 inches tall*

*Plate: 310*
*Title: Girls*
*Artist: L. Chulkova*
*Size: 5-piece, 6 inches tall*

labels glued on, but these have long since disappeared. Nevertheless, unusual dolls do exist, such as the Mari-El doll from the 1970s shown in Chapter 5.

Michele Lyons Lefkowitz's book, *A Collector's Guide to Nesting Dolls,* provides an invaluable guide to the variety of dolls produced during the Soviet period. Furthermore, even traditional dolls have evolved over the years, so a factory doll from the 1940s or 1950s can have an appeal of its own. The Artistic-Pedagogical Museum of Toys in Sergiev Posad shows a traditional doll made in 1959, for example, that has a slightly more primitive, but endearing air than its sisters of today, despite sharing the same design.

As discussed in Chapter 1, there was still substantial variety in the dolls made in the 1920s; dolls from this era and earlier are typically museum pieces. If you are a committed collector and have the opportunity to purchase one of these dolls, you are very fortunate.

## Where to Buy

There are more than twenty reliable importers of matryoshki in the United States,

*Plate: 311*
*Title: Russian Fairytales*
*Artist: A. Gavrilenko*
*Size: 5-piece, 6 inches tall*
*Andrei Gavrilenko combines illustrations of Russian fairy tales with text written to simulate old Russian script. The only front side shown in this plate is the outermost doll, in the center of the upper row. Behind it is the backside. The rest are all backsides of the dolls. The illustrations include* Ivan and Vasilisa on the Gray Wolf*; a bogatyr (mythical hero of early Russian history);* Baba Yaga, *the ugly witch riding in her bucket and carrying her broom;* Ivan Tsarevich and the Frog Princess; *and* The Goose Swans.

almost all of whom work with retail stores. Considerable information about many of these importers can be found on the internet.

The stores themselves range from gift stores to book stores to toy stores. Nesting dolls can also be found at craft fairs, either local or with an international theme. Not surprisingly, stores in expensive locations will charge more for their dolls. However, these are often the stores with the higher end dolls, so you will have to decide if you are willing to pay the mark-up. If you are building an extensive collection, you can develop relationships directly with the importers.

## Izmailovo

Serious collectors should consider visiting Russia, and in particular the Izmailovo market in Moscow, which is the center of matryoshka marketing. Located in the northeastern section of the city, it is a large open-air fair for arts, crafts, and antiques. Most tourists refer to it by the name of the region of Moscow in which it is located—Izmailovo. Russians in the business refer to it as the *vernissage,* which denotes the opening of an art show. At the Izmailovsky Park metro stop is a large, wooded park and a hotel complex, as well as a market for household goods and inexpensive clothing.

The Izmailovo market is open all week long, but most business is done on Wednesdays and weekends. In the early years, Izmailovo operated only on weekends, with a small group of artists who also displayed their work on Fridays. Friday evolved into "wholesale day," which was little different from weekends, except that buyers could negotiate small discounts for large quantities. Wholesale day then moved to Thursdays, starting at 6:00 pm, and buyers shopped in the dark. Then wholesale hours were moved, for inexplicable reasons, to midnight on Wednesdays. As of this writing, trade buying begins on Wednesday at 8:00 am.

The market keeps growing and has acquired an imposing structure; not only are dilapidated metal stalls from the early 1990s being replaced by attractive wooden booths, but the entire market is beginning to resemble a kremlin, with walls and several towers. Nevertheless, Izmailovo remains oddly inconvenient to buyers. A major challenge in the winter is to stay warm long enough to complete one's shopping. Snacks and resting facilities are extremely limited and inefficient. It is difficult to imagine how the vendors survive the long days.

A trip to Sergiev Posad would be worthwhile, although it is rare to find an unusual nesting doll there; the independent artists from Sergiev Posad usually sell through their distributors or at Izmailovo. The very first Russian matryoshka is located in Sergiev Posad in the Artistic-Pedagogical Museum of Toys. Their entire matryoshka exhibit, however, fills only one case.

If you visit St. Petersburg, the major market is just off Nevsky Prospect, behind the Cathedral

*Plate: 312 (opposite, top)*
*The alleys of Izmailovo market are lined with charming wooden booths with awnings that keep the weather off buyers–a bit.*

*Plate: 313 (opposite, bottom)*
*The booths of Izmailovo are a seemingly endless array of matryoshki, arts, and crafts.*

*Plate: 314 (overleaf)*
*Title: My Tale for You*
*Artist: O. Sarzevskaya*
*Size: 10-piece, 12 inches tall*

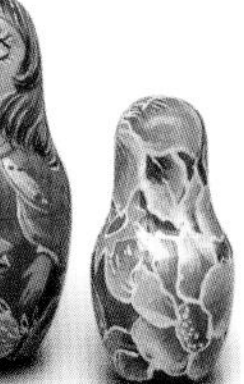

*Plate: 315*
*Title: Girls in Flowers*
*Artist: E. Fabianskaya*
*Size: 7-piece, 7 inches tall*
*This is the popular flower matryoshka taken to the highest level.*

*Plate: 316*
*Title: Magical Clouds*
*Artist: E. Fabianskaya*
*Size: 7-piece, 8 inches tall*

*Plate: 317*
*Title: Stories and Plays by William Shakespeare*
*Artist: M. Streltsova*
*Size: 7-piece, 8 inches tall*
*Masha Streltsova's interpretations of Shakespeare's works include wonderful abstractions to help convey the characters' state of mind.*

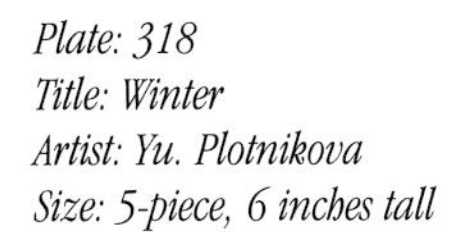

*Plate: 318*
*Title: Winter*
*Artist: Yu. Plotnikova*
*Size: 5-piece, 6 inches tall*

*Plate: 319*
*Title: Old Scotland Fest*
*Artist: Ye. Semyonova*
*Size: 7-piece, 6 inches tall*

of the Savior of the Blood.

Keep your eyes open on side trips. Some of my most interesting purchases have been at small stores far from the normal production centers and outlets. In any case, if you are contemplating a trip to Russia, you should consider talking to one of the importers and possibly finding someone who can help you with your purchases while you are in Russia.

*Plate: 320*
*Title: In the Garden*
*Artist: Yu. Kovaleva*
*Size: 7-piece, 9 inches tall*
*Yulia Kovaleva's art is reminiscent of Russian artists of the early 20th century such as Petrov-Vodkin and Kustodiev.*

## Symbols Within Symbols

The history of matryoshki closely mirrors Russia's recent history. Matryoshki were born during the attempts in the 1890s to industrialize yet maintain Russia's cultural roots. During the Soviet period, when the Communist party attempted to control all political and economic life, matryoshki were mass produced, with no allowance for individual creativity. The demise of the Soviet Union has allowed Russians to regain their personal freedom, and has led to a flowering of matryoshka artists and entrepreneurs. Not only are matryoshki dolls within dolls; they have become symbols within symbols. Collecting matryoshki is a way to participate in this still evolving history, as today's matryoshka artists create the next chapter.

*Plate: 321*
*Title: The Scarlet Flower*
*Artist: Yu. Plotnikova*
*Size: 10-piece, 10 inches tall*
*Yulia Plotnikova's work is more traditional than that of most of the Abramtsevo artists. This doll includes features found on fine matryoshka dolls—a face on top and a medallion illustrating a Russian fairy tale—executed beautifully.*

*Plate: 322 (opposite)*
*Title: Mordovian Doll*
*City: Mordovia*
*Size: 5-piece, 5 inches tall*
*Collection: Rett and Tania Ertl*
*This doll was purchased in the 1970s.*

*Plate: 323 (above)*
*Title: Antique Eggs (c.1900s)*
*City: Sergiev Posad*
*Size: 3-piece, 4 inches tall*
*From a private collection.*

*Plate: 324 (left)*
*Title: Satire on a Priest (c.1920s)*
*Artist: V. I. Sokolov*
*Size: 3-piece, 5 inches tall*
*From a private collection.*

*Plate: 325 (overleaf)*
*Title: Family of the Last Russian Tsar*
*City: Rostov-on-Don*
*Artist: L. G. Saprikina*
*Size: 7 pieces, 7 inches tall*
*Collection: The Russian Shop, Lisle, Illinois*
*Tsar Nicholas II with his heir, Tsarevich Aleksei, followed by Tsaritsa Aleksandra and their daughters: Olga, Tatiana, Marie, and Anastasia. The back of each doll is enhanced by a Russian double-headed eagle, the Romanov family crest.*

# Appendix

# Annotated Bibliography

## Nonfiction

Filippova, Elena. *Russian Matrjoshka*. Moscow: no date. 108 pages.

A collection of photographs of matryoshki painted by artists from the Abramtsevo school of artists.

Gorozhanina, S. V. "K istorii khudozhestvennoi obrabotki dereva v tekhnike vyzhiganii," in *Sergievo-posadskii muzei-zapovednik*. Moscow: Izdatel'stvo "PIK," 1995. pp. 283–299.

A chapter on the history of wood burning techniques used in the late nineteenth century.

Gorozhanina, S. V. "K istorii tokarnogo promysla Sergieva Posada XIX–XX veka," in *Nauchnye chteniya pamyati V. M. Vasilenko*. Moscow: Vserosiiskii muzei dekorativno-prikladnogo i narodnogo iskusstva, 1998. pp. 118–127.

A chapter from an academic collection dealing with the art of turning in Sergiev Posad in the eighteenth and nineteenth centuries.

Gorozhanina, S. V. "Zemskie khudozhestvennye masterskie," in O. V. Kruglova, ed., *Russkoye narodnoye iskusstva*. Moscow: Izdatelskii dom "Podkova," 1998. pp. 146–165.

A chapter that describes the workshops of Sergiev Posad in the nineteenth century.

*Hampelmann & Matrjoschka*—Holzspielzeug aus Deutschland und Russland. Kassel: Wintershall AG, 1998. 223 pages.

A catalog published in conjunction with an exhibit in Kassel, which took place from November 29, 1998, through January 31, 1999. The exhibit was sponsored by the German company Wintershall AG and the Russian company OAO Gazprom.

*Plate: 326 (appendix title)*
*Title: Stacked Workpieces*
*Factory: Art Alliance, Kirov*
*Logs cut into workpieces are stacked, ready to be put onto the lathes for turning.*

*Plate: 327 (opposite)*
*Title: The Mermaid*
*Artist: M. Streltsova*
*Size: 7-piece, 8 inches tall*

Hilton, Alison. *Russian Folk Art*. Bloomington: Indiana University Press, 1995. 350 pages.

Most of a chapter is devoted to the Abramtsevo artist colony, an important breeding ground for the first matryoshki and for some of the most exquisite matryoshki being produced today.

Lefkovitz, Michele Lyons. *A Collector's Guide to Nesting Dolls: Histories, Identification, Values*. Florence, Ala.: Books Americana, 1989. 173 pages.

The most extensive book on the regional differences of dolls produced during the Soviet period. It also includes photos and descriptions of nesting dolls from other countries. Most of the photographs are black and white.

Maxym, Lucy. *Russian Lacquer, Legends, and Fairy Tales*. Manhasset, N.Y.: Siamese Imports Co., 1981. 80 pages.

The definitive American book about traditional Russian lacquer boxes, describing each of the four villages where they are produced: Fedoskino, Palekh, Kholui, and Mstyora. These boxes provide many of the images that are painted on medallions of matryoshki. The book uses the boxes to illustrate short versions of Russian tales, so it is a good place to find synopses of famous tales.

Obryvalin, A. and Tyurin, Yu. (eds.). *Matryoshka, Russian Souvenir*. Moscow: Sovetskaya Rossiya, 1969. 108 pages.

This is a small format book with photographs of many unusual historical matryoshki, including the early period as well as the Soviet period. Interestingly, L. Soloviova (see below) is listed as the foreign proofreader.

Soloviova, L. N. *Matryoshka*. Moscow: Interbook Business, 1997. 96 pages.

Ms. Soloviova is the director of the Moscow Museum of Matryoshki.

Soloviova, Larissa, and Marina Marder. *Russian Matryoshka*. Moscow: Interbook, 1993. 64 pages.

The first modern Russian hard-backed book about matryoshki, it features a description of the various regions and the dolls produced in those regions. Ms. Marder is the founder of an import business, which she later sold.

## Children's Books

Bliss, Corinne Demas. *The Littlest Matryoshka*. New York: Hyperion, 1999. 32 pages.

The story of a little girl who buys a small nesting doll whose middle piece has been lost in the store. The little girl takes special care of each piece of the doll. The book follows the journey of the smallest piece into the snow, onto a snowplow, down a river, and then plucked from the water by a great blue heron, which finally returns the doll to the house where the little girl lives, reuniting the smallest piece with her sisters. This is clearly an American book, as it features a "happy ending," an ending that occurs less often in Russian stories.

Ogburn, Jacqueline. *The Magic Nesting Doll*. New York: Dial Press, 2000. 32 pages.

A beautifully illustrated story that turns *Sleeping Beauty* on its head. A little girl's grandmother presents her with a nesting doll, telling her to open it only in case of extreme need. The little girl hears about a prince who is frozen and goes to visit him. The prince is guarded by his uncle, a grand vizier, who does not want the girl to interfere in his affairs and tells his men to throw the girl in the dungeon. The girl opens the nesting doll, and a bear appears to help her get out of the dungeon. The villain uncle then banishes her to the forest, where the girl opens the next doll and is saved by a wolf. Finally, the grand vizier's men throw the girl down a cliff, where she opens the last piece and is saved by a firebird. The girl goes back to the prince. The grand vizier is then frozen and the prince thawed out. The prince falls in love with the girl, and they live happily ever after.

Van Allsburg, Chris. *The Polar Express*. Boston: Houghton Mifflin Company, 1985. 32 pages.

A wonderful story about a boy who takes the Polar Express to visit Santa at the North Pole on Christmas Eve. Santa selects the boy to receive the first gift of Christmas, and he asks Santa for a bell off his sleigh. When the boy arrives home that night, he has lost the bell. On Christmas morning, however, the last gift the boy receives is the bell, which has been found and wrapped up by Santa. TolsToys created a nesting doll featuring illustrations from the book, with active help from the author and publisher.

# Glossary of English and Russian Terms

**Abramtsevo,** the estate owned by Savva and Elizaveta Mamontov, where they created the most famous Russian artist colony of the 19th century. It is just a few minutes from Sergiev Posad. It was here that Sergei Malyutin directed the workshop to teach peasants woodworking.

**Artel,** a combination of a workshop and factory; artists could either do their work here or bring their work from home. Many of the early matryoshka workshops were *artels.* Several *artels* have appeared recently, although the name is not being used.

**Babushka,** the Russian word for grandmother; a nesting doll that opens to three smaller dolls, which in turn open to three tiny dolls, for a total of thirteen. The term is also used erroneously in place of the term matryoshka.

**Biryulki,** a game involving picking up small wooden pieces with a hook, and then dropping them into a cup. The pieces are produced on a lathe, as are matryoshka dolls.

**Bogatyr,** a knight-errant. These men, the subject of Russian legends, are often pictured on matryoshki, usually wearing pointed hats.

**Guberniya,** a political division in pre-revolutionary Russia, roughly equivalent to an American state. Since 1917, they have been called *oblast.*

**Izmailovo,** the location of the main craft market in Moscow, near the wooded park and the metro station named for it, Izmailovsky Park.

**Khotkovo,** a village near Sergiev Posad. The home of many matryoshka painters.

**Kolobok,** a bun. It is an archaic Russian word, but is the name of a well known folk tale. The story is similar to the American *Gingerbread Boy.*

**Korobeinik,** a doll that looks like a matryoshka from the outside, but that actually has several figures inside – usually Christmas ornaments.

**Mesto,** the Russian word for place, it is also the word used for each piece of a matryoshka. Thus, a 5-piece doll would have 5 *mest.* (In the plural, the "o" is dropped.)

**Museum of Matryoshki** (Moscow), a relatively new museum, housed in the Museum of Folk Art near the TASS building in Moscow.

**Nevalyashka,** a type of doll that does not open, but rather has a bell inside. It is shaped like a bell or light bulb, and is weighted so that it will not fall over. In English, this doll has various names, including bell, roly-poly, and weeble.

**Oblast,** a political subdivision in the Soviet Union, and now in Russia, roughly equivalent to an American state. Named for the largest city of the *oblast,* some of the best known include Moscow oblast, Kirov oblast, and Nizhegorodskaya (Nizhny Novgorod) oblast, all of which are home to matryoshka factories.

**Perekupchik,** literally, a rebuyer. The derogatory term for a middleman, still used by Russian people who believe that businesspeople should not profit from artists' work.

**Potal,** a foil applied to a nesting doll, giving the appearance of gold or silver leaf.

**Samouchka,** one who is self-taught, specifically an artist who is not professionally trained. From the root *samo,* "self" and *uchit',* "to teach."

**Skazka,** a fairy tale or a folk tale.

**Trinity-Sergiev Monastery** (Sergievskaya-Troitskaya Lavra), the large monastery in the center of Sergiev Posad. It was founded in the 13th century by St. Sergius of Radonezh, for whom Sergiev Posad is named. The seminary in the monastery continued to operate throughout the Soviet period, and it remains the principal monastery of the Russian Orthodox Church.

**Troika,** a vehicle pulled by three horses, either a carriage or a sleigh. Often portrayed in Russian art and nesting dolls.

**Tsarevich,** a tsar's son. Most often encountered as Tsarevich Ivan, the mythical third son of the tsar in the fairy tale *The Frog Princess.* Ivan is the youngest son, and is fated to marry a frog that turns into a princess during the day. When he burns the frog's skin, the princess is taken away, and Ivan spends much of his life looking for the princess.

**Tsarevna,** a tsar's daughter or the wife of a tsarevich. The best known is the *Frog Tsarevna,* usually translated as *The Frog Princess.*

*Plate: 328 (below)*
*Title: Our Little Town*
*Artist: E. Saifulmulukov*
*Size: 5-piece, 6 inches tall*

росписи Жуков Дмитрий

# INDEX

Index entries in roman text indicate the page number; *italic* numbers indicate the page of a caption; **boldface** entries indicate plate numbers. Matryoshka titles and Russian words are in italics.



*Plate: 329 (opposite)*
*Title: Girls*
*Artist: Dm. Zhukov*
*Size: 9-piece, 7 inches tall*

## Photography

Photographs of matryoshki, the cities, and factories in *The Art of the Russian Matryoshka* are by Rick Hibberd except for the following: The artists portraits and studio still-life photos on pages 157-180 are by Moscow photographer Yakov Chitov, also his are plate numbers **001, 004, 011, 019, 021, 022, 120, 144, 166, 199, 295-311, 314-321, 323, 324, 327, 327-330**; the interiors and still-life photos of Factory No.1 on pages 128-129 are by TolsToys's St. Petersburg partner Denis Tolstoy; historical photos of Sergiev Posad, plates **009, 010, 012, 013, 015-017, 020, 023-026**, and **067** are courtesy of the Sergiev Posad Artistic-Pedagogical Museum of Toys of the Russian Academy of Education and the Sergiev Posad Museum of Applied Folk Art; plate numbers **147** and **325** are courtesy of The Russian Shop, Lisle, Illinois.

## Colophon

This text of the book is set in Garamond with Garamond Light Italic captions. The fonts are modern adaptations of designs by printer, publisher, and type designer Claude Garamond, whose sixteenth-century types were modeled on those of Venetian printers from the end of the previous century. Headlines and subheads are Weiss Roman. Photograph scanning, printing, and binding was done by Dai Nippon (DNP America, Inc.), with manufacturing facilities in Hong Kong.

*Plate: 330 (above)*
*Title: Men from Zaporozhets*
*Artist: N. D. Bartram*
*Size: 8-piece, 8 inches tall*
*Collection: Museum of Applied Folk Art (1910s).*